CW00341200

Achieving Global Open Access

Achieving Global Open Access explores some of the key conditions that are necessary to deliver global Open Access (OA) that is effective and equitable.

Often assumed to be a self-evident good, OA has been subject to growing criticism for perpetuating global inequities and epistemic injustices. It has been seen as imposing exploitative business and publishing models and as exacerbating exclusionary research evaluation cultures and practices. Pinfield engages with these issues, recognising that the global OA debate is now not just about publishing business models and academic reward structures, but also about what constitutes valid and valuable knowledge, how we know, and who gets to say. The book argues that, for OA to deliver its potential, it first needs to be associated with 'epistemic openness', a wider and more inclusive understanding of what constitutes valid and valuable knowledge. It also needs to be accompanied by 'participatory openness', enabling contributions to knowledge from more diverse communities. Interacting with relevant theory and current practice, the book discusses the challenges in implementing these different forms of openness, the relationships between them, and their limits.

Achieving Global Open Access is essential reading for academics and students engaged in the study of Library and Information Science, Open Access and Publishing. It will also be valuable and interesting to library and publishing professionals around the world.

Stephen Pinfield is Professor of Information Services Management at the University of Sheffield, UK, and a Senior Research Fellow at the Research on Research Institute. He has a particular interest in scholarly communication, open science, and research policy. He has been involved in national and international policy development in these areas, and the creation of open systems and services, since the early 2000s. He was the founding Director of Sherpa from 2002 to 2012, an initiative managing projects and providing services to support the global open access community.

Routledge Critical Studies on Open Access

This new and thought-provoking series will provide researchers, students, policymakers and practitioners with the latest critical thinking on Open Access. With contributions from international experts, titles in the series will be relevant to those working in a wide range of disciplines, including library, archival and information science, media studies, communication studies and publishing studies.

The following list includes only the most recent titles published within the series. A list of the full catalogue of titles is available at: https://www.routledge.com/Routledge-Critical-Studies-on-Open-Access/book-series/RCSOA

Open Access in Theory and Practice
The Theory-Practice Relationship and Openness
Stephen Pinfield, Simon Wakeling, David Bawden, Lyn Robinson

Achieving Global Open Access
The Need for Scientific, Epistemic and Participatory Openness
Stephen Pinfield

Achieving Global Open Access

The Need for Scientific, Epistemic and Participatory Openness

Stephen Pinfield

Routledge
Taylor & Francis Group

LONDON AND NEW YORK

First published 2025
by Routledge
4 Park Square, Milton Park, Abingdon, Oxon OX14 4RN

and by Routledge
605 Third Avenue, New York, NY 10158

*Routledge is an imprint of the Taylor & Francis Group, an
informa business*

British Library Cataloguing-in-Publication Data
A catalogue record for this book is available from the
British Library

ISBN: 978-1-032-62575-1 (hbk)
ISBN: 978-1-032-67926-6 (pbk)
ISBN: 978-1-032-67925-9 (ebk)

DOI: 10.4324/9781032679259

Typeset in Times New Roman
by MPS Limited, Dehradun

Contents

Acknowledgements

In many respects, this book has been a long time in the making, since it draws together several strands of work in which I have been involved over a number of years. I would like to thank all the colleagues I have worked with over that time from whom I have learned so much. That is not to say that my colleagues have always agreed with my ideas, or that they will agree with all the ideas in this book, but I have often learned as much from respectful disagreements as anything else.

Colleagues with whom I have worked on recent research projects have influenced my thinking in innumerable ways and I would like to thank them for that. Colleagues in the Research on Research Institute (RoRI) have taught me a great deal, particularly Ludo Waltman, Helen Buckley Woods, Wolfgang Kaltenbrunner, James Wilsdon, Johanna Brumberg, Susana Oliveira Henriques and Narmin Rzayeva. Thanks to them and other RoRI colleagues. From the VOICES project, I would like to thank Melanie Benson Marshall, Pamela Abbott, Andrew Cox, Juan Pablo Alperin, Germana Barata, Natascha Chtena, Isabelle Dorsch, Alice Fleerackers, Monique Oliveira, and Isabella Peters. Whilst these colleagues have not input directly into this book, and they may disagree with some of it, I have gained an enormous amount from their knowledge and expertise, and I count it a privilege to be working with them. I would also like to thank colleagues at the University of Sheffield with whom I have previously worked on open access projects, Peter Bath and Peter Willett.

I would like to thank Simon Wakeling for his comments on a very early version of the arguments in this book. His frank and constructive criticisms made a big difference in my thinking at that preliminary stage and were very influential in the direction this book has taken. More generally, Simon has had a significant input into my thinking on open access in all sorts of ways.

I owe a great intellectual debt to advocates and thinkers who have worked on open access over the last 20 years. Some of them I know well, others not so much, but I have gained a great deal from all of them in various ways. In particular, I would like to thank Bill Hubbard, Jenny Fry, Rob Johnson, Bo-Christer Björk, Leslie Chan, Jean-Claude Guédon, Stevan Harnad, Cameron Neylon, Florence Piron, Peter Suber, and John Willinsky.

I benefited a great deal from comments from two peer reviewers of this book. Thanks to them for their very helpful and challenging feedback.

I had completed an early draft of this book before Sabina Leonelli's excellent book, *Philosophy of Open Science*, was published. I was, however, able to take her work into account in the process of extending and redrafting this book. She also gave me extremely helpful comments on a more mature draft of this book, for which I am very grateful.

I received useful advice from University Library staff at the University of Sheffield about making this book open access and financial support for payment of the book processing charge. I am very grateful.

The writing of this book was completed while I was on research leave from my role at the University of Sheffield. Thanks to the Faculty of Social Sciences at Sheffield for granting me research leave during the first semester of the 2023–24 academic year. Thanks to Val Gillet, who, as Head of School, supported my application.

I spent much of my research leave as a visiting scholar in Oxford during the Michaelmas term in 2023. My thanks go to Richard Ovenden, Bodley's Librarian, and his colleagues for welcoming me and giving me office space in the Weston Library as a visiting scholar. The Weston was an ideal working environment during my time in Oxford. Thanks to Alexandra Franklin, who oversees the Visiting Scholars' Centre, for her welcome and support.

Thanks also to the Rector, Henry Woudhuysen, and Fellows of Lincoln College Oxford, who elected me an Associate Member of the Senior Common Room, allowing me to take part in College life during that term. I am grateful for their welcome and for the many stimulating conversations I had with members of the SCR, which at the same time enlarged my thinking and helped me to focus on the work of writing.

Finally, thanks to my family for their endless love and support – they are such a wonderful blessing. My daughter, Joanna, and my son, Edward, have always helped me to put things into perspective and focus on what is most important in life. They are a joy. My wife, Valerie, has given me more love, support, and encouragement than I can ever say, and it is to her that I dedicate this book, with love and thanks.

Abbreviations

APC	Article Processing Charge
BOAI	Budapest Open Access Initiative
BOAI@20	Budapest Open Access Initiative 20th anniversary recommendations
CRediT	Contributor Roles Taxonomy
CV	Curriculum Vitae
DORA	Declaration on Research Assessment
HICs	High-Income Countries
HSS	Humanities and Social Sciences
INASP	International Network for Advancing Science and Policy
IT	Information Technology
LMICs	Low- and Middle-Income Countries
OA	Open Access
OECD	Organization for Economic Cooperation and Development
OS	Open Science
RedALyC	Red de Revistas Científicas de América Latina y El Caribe
SciELO	Scientific Electronic Library
SDGs	Strategic Development Goals
STEMM	Science, Technology, Engineering, Mathematics, and Medicine
TMSA	Transformational Model of Social Action
UNESCO	United Nations Educational, Scientific and Cultural Organization
WHO	World Health Organisation
WoS	Web of Science

Foreword

At the outset, I want to mention two related things: my motivations for writing this book and my recognition of my own positionality. I want to be clear right from the beginning about the personal context for my remarks and the perspective it gives me. I will explore both the importance and the limits of relying on good intentions and personal standpoints later in this book, but highlighting these things in my own case now will help to introduce what I am hoping to contribute with this book.

I am writing from the perspective of a long-standing advocate of open access (OA), whose ideas have developed in the process of creating, using, and evaluating open access systems and policies since the beginning of the 21st century. That the results of research should be openly available so that they can be used by others has always seemed obvious to me, particularly when the research is sponsored by governments and charities who fund it as a public good. However, over the last twenty years or more, I have seen criticism of and opposition to open access come from different places. Commonly, the criticism and opposition have come from people with a vested interest in the conventional scholarly communication system and its business models – commercial publishers, journal editors, senior members of learned societies, and so on. Over the years, I have been involved in addressing many of those criticisms. However, more recently, criticism of open access, and sometimes opposition to it, has come from people who have usually been seen as its potential beneficiaries – people in smaller institutions in high-income countries (HICs) and people in low-and-middle-income countries (LMICs). This is challenging, to say the least. Some of the very people we assumed would welcome open access are criticising, even opposing, it. This book has been written as a way of seriously listening to and carefully engaging with some key aspects of that more recent criticism and opposition.

My perspective is based, of course, on my positionality: on my own identity, rooted in my immediate environment. I am a researcher and teacher based in a UK research-intensive University, and a former information services professional involved in developing open access policies and services. I have been working on OA in one form or another for much of my career. I have been involved in setting up OA services and developed OA policies in institutions, and I have also played a role in national and international developments in various ways. Any contribution I will make in this book comes from that experience and perspective. It will, of course, also be made in the context of my personal identity – white, male, middle-aged, advantaged.

Recognising my own positionality is crucial in engaging in what Kathleen Fitzpatrick (2019) calls "generous thinking". Generous thinking, I believe, is crucial in the field of openness, especially as OA can give rise to strong opinions. A major component of such generosity is listening, as Fitzpatrick says. Listening is itself a key aspect of humility, something I see as a pre-condition for meaningful dialogue, and something emphasised by Naomi Oreskes (2019) to be an essential part of trustworthy science. Therefore, as part of preparing to write this book, I have tried to listen to and engage with a variety of voices. I have read as widely as I can, and I have taken part in numerous discussions in different parts of the world. I have continued to work with a variety of partners on making OA a reality in a way that is both effective and equitable. All that is still ongoing. So, this book is intended to be part of a continuing conversation, which involves listening, reflecting, responding, and listening again.

Indeed, part of the argument of this book is that we need to create an environment where we can hear a more diverse range of voices and engage with more perspectives – open access can contribute to such an environment, I believe. I will suggest in what follows that open access itself can become a manifestation of generous thinking, as Fitzpatrick argues it should be, in that it involves sharing and interaction. However, if it is to work at a global level, open access needs to change, in some respects, radically. We need to consider carefully how open access systems and services are set up and how they can be made as effective and equitable as possible. What we need to change, as well as what we need to keep, are the subject of this book.

References

Fitzpatrick, K. (2019). *Generous thinking: A radical approach to saving the university*. Johns Hopkins University Press.
Oreskes, N. (2019). *Why trust science?* Princeton University Press.

1 Introduction

In this book, I want to explore some of the key conditions that are necessary to deliver global open access in a way that is effective and equitable. I will argue that alongside open access to research literature and other forms of openness in science (which I will call 'scientific openness') additional kinds of openness are required. I want to make the case for what I will call 'epistemic openness' and 'participatory openness'. I will introduce these concepts in a moment, and then go on in the rest of this book to explore them in more detail and discuss their relationship with open access.

Open access (OA) exists where the outputs of research are "digital, online, free of charge, and free of most copyright and licensing restrictions" (Suber, 2012, p. 4). OA has often been assumed to be a self-evident common good. The dissemination of scientific research (using 'scientific research' in the widest possible way to cover all academic disciplines) is often seen as a source of global benefits, and so, making the science publishing system as open as possible becomes a global imperative (Drake et al., 2023). Ensuring the findings of research are communicated as rapidly and widely as possible to an international audience creates benefits for the scientific community, accelerating scientific progress, and for society more generally, enabling the latest science to be put to use by clinicians, entrepreneurs, policymakers, and others (Ola, 2018; Willinsky, 2006).

However, in the last decade, open access has been subject to growing criticism. OA has been attributed with creating, perpetuating, or exacerbating global inequities. It has been seen as imposing exploitative business and publishing models on researchers in low-resource contexts, particularly, low- and middle-income countries (LMICs). OA has been criticised as intensifying exclusionary research evaluation cultures and practices, which keep scholars from the Global South at the periphery. It has also been characterised as a form of neo-colonial hegemonic power which generates epistemic injustice. OA, it is argued, is responsible for

DOI: 10.4324/9781032679259-1

strengthening the domination of Western knowledge systems, such as conventional science, and helping to marginalise indigenous knowledge forms. Rather than being any kind of solution to global inequity, open access has been seen as part of the problem.

In his critical analysis of the current state of global open access, Knöchelmann (2021) identifies many models of OA launched in the Global North as ones which "reinforce imperialist structures that are morally disguised" (p. 75). Although OA publishing is often presented as "better publishing", Knöchelmann argues that in fact it widens access to scholarship from the Global North and crowds out other forms of knowledge, acting as a kind of epistemic colonialism. Similarly, Mboa Nkoudou (2020) states that "OA now often seems to reinforce and to create new inequalities", particularly in Africa, where OA "acts as a poison that causes epistemicides and linguicides in Africa and whose most insidious manifestation is epistemic alienation" (p. 26). Piron (2018) refers to OA as a "tool of neocolonialism" (p. 118). Sengupta (2021) argues that "OA entrenches prevailing 'academic colonialism'" and furthers "deep-seeded [sic] exclusion and discrimination" (p. 203). OA has an amplifying effect on research outputs from the Global North which has reached such a volume that it drowns out other voices. These and other similar critiques of OA add up to a considerable challenge for OA advocates.

In this book, I want to interact with these kinds of criticisms of the global implications of OA, as well as myself critiquing some current approaches to OA. I will argue that if open access is to deliver its potential globally, first, it needs to be accompanied by a wider and more inclusive understanding of what constitutes valid and valuable knowledge ('epistemic openness'); and second, it needs to enable interactions involving more diverse communities ('participatory openness'). I will explore the relationships between these different forms of openness, and also some of their limits, in what follows.

I am using the word 'openness' to describe these different things to emphasise the close association between scientific, epistemic, and participatory openness, and because they all have in common the removal of barriers and constraints. 'Openness' involves notions of transparency and collaboration. It also connotes free enquiry, and receptivity to new ideas and influences. 'Openness' is used in a wide range of contexts which have in common these kinds of ideas. For example, "open government" describes moves to make political and administrative decision-making more transparent (Ingrams, 2020). "Trade openness" is used as a description of economic relations where there are minimal barriers to trade (Montalbano, 2011). "Openness to experience" is used in psychology to describe a personality trait associated with receptivity to newness and others (Connelly et al.,

2014). Of course, these different kinds of openness are not without their own problems, in theory and practice, but my point is that conceptually they involve ideas such as transparency, inclusivity, and receptivity. I am using 'openness' in 'scientific openness', 'epistemic openness', and 'participatory openness' to convey those ideas in ways that I will explore as this book progresses. 'Openness' should not, therefore, be seen as something that is just passive – simply the absence of barriers and constraints. Rather, I am using 'openness' to describe something active and dynamic.

The case I will make will have wide-ranging practical implications, for OA systems and services, and for the policies and strategies that underpin them. As well as discussing practice, it will also be necessary to interact with theory – particularly social, economic, and cultural theories that have been applied to global OA, and, in some cases, used to critique it. These include critical theory, postcolonial theory, commons theory, as well as others. I will also engage with relevant questions of meta-theory, which undergirds social, economic, and cultural theories used to discuss OA. In fact, I will suggest that opposing positions taken by, on the one hand, many advocates of OA, and, on the other hand, its critics, have often been based on meta-theoretical differences. Important though these fundamental differences are, they are usually left unacknowledged and undiscussed. Differences about what constitutes reality and our knowledge of it, and of what counts as valid and valuable knowledge, and who gets to say, often underpin different positions on OA. Debates about openness are commonly at source debates about knowledge itself. When left unacknowledged, such differences typically mean that OA advocates and critics talk past one another without finding the language or concepts to engage with each other's arguments. Nevertheless, I will contend, it is essential to try to engage and to navigate a path through these ideas. The ideas in question impact significantly on our understanding of the importance of knowledge generated as part of research, which then itself informs our under-standing of the role of open access. The theory, I will argue, has significant implications for open access policies and practices.

Open access and open science

Making openness work in relation to 'scholarly communication' (how researchers communicate their research findings) has gained increasing prominence since the early 2000s, although its origins can be traced back considerably further (Moore, 2017, 2019). OA developments have tended to focus on peer-reviewed articles published in journals, the primary vehicle for scholarly communication for most disciplines. The idea of the journal, as a regularly published collection of articles in particular fields of research, is a core part of the established scholarly communication system taken for granted by most researchers. One key role of journals has traditionally been managing peer review – the quality assurance process where independent experts assess an output. Journal editors and publishers organise the peer review process for submitted articles, and then use it as the basis for 'accept' or 'reject' decisions for their journals, as well as a means of improving papers before publication. Peer review is a highly valued part of scholarly communication as a way of maintaining the quality of scientific outputs (Mulligan et al., 2013; Nicholas et al., 2015), often seen as "the cornerstone of scientific publishing integrity" (Hillard & Baber, 2021, p. 107). At the same time, peer review comes with widely discussed problems, including, as Smith (2006) puts it, that it is "slow, expensive, profligate of academic time, highly subjective, something of a lottery, prone to bias, and easily abused" (p. 179). Partly due to problems such as these, the role and value of both peer review and the journal have been increasingly debated over recent years, and those debates have often, although not always, been tied up with debates about open access (Waltman et al., 2022). Both the role of the journal and peer review will come into consideration at key points in our exploration of global open access in this book. Of course, open access can also apply to other published research outputs, such as conference proceedings, books, chapters from books, and similar artefacts, which may be more or less important in different disciplines. The process of publishing such outputs normally also involves peer review or editorial quality assurance. However, the robustness and rigour of such processes will vary, as with journals.

Various modes of implementing open access have been developed over the last three decades, and I will go on in a moment to provide a provisional outline of them. The rest of this book will then fill out the details, exploring the global implications of these different modes of OA more fully. However, it is worth pointing out at this early stage just how controversial even quite well-established approaches to OA are. Different actors – researchers, funders, publishers, librarians, university managers, and others – working in different organisations, representing different disciplines, and based in different countries all contribute to an ongoing debate. There is a wide range of radically different views on OA, both across and within different actor groups. OA is still a highly contested issue, and ongoing contestation is an important backdrop to this book.

The practice of sharing OA copies of outputs, such as articles, either before or after peer review (or both), has been practised by some research communities for decades. High-energy physicists set up the arXiv server for sharing preprints (versions of articles before they have been peer reviewed) as far back as 1991. arXiv now contains both pre- and post-peer-reviewed versions of papers – over 2.3 million outputs in total – and is used by mathematicians, computer scientists and others. Nevertheless, preprinting remains highly controversial or largely ignored in many other disciplinary communities. The arXiv server is still exceptional in the OA landscape as a preprint server the use of which is part of accepted practice in its core disciplinary communities. Other disciplinary preprint servers have been set up, many of them as part of a "second wave" of servers since 2015 (Chiarelli et al., 2019), and their usage is growing, but remains at very low levels compared with physicists' use of arXiv.

Many research-performing institutions worldwide have also established OA repositories, encouraging researchers within their institutions to deposit copies of their outputs (Bashir et al., 2021). Usage of such repositories varies enormously, typically related to the institutional, funder, or national policy environments in which they operate. Where robust policies are in place, encouraging or requiring the deposit of outputs, rates of OA tend to rise markedly (Larivière & Sugimoto, 2018). Some countries or even global regions have set up OA repositories, including RINarxiv for Indonesia and AfricArXiv for Africa. However, contributions to these kinds of archives from researchers often remain low. Despite the growth in available preprint servers and other repositories, the usage of such venues is still not part of customary practice for many researchers.

Whilst the depositing of copies of papers in repositories or servers (an approach known as 'green' OA) runs alongside the journal publishing process, interacting with it at different points, some models of OA have been developed which allow articles to be published in an OA form in journals themselves ('gold' OA). Fully OA journals have been published since the 1990s. A new business model for OA journals replacing the traditional subscription model was established by some gold OA journals in the early 2000s. It involves payment of article processing charges (APCs) by the author, their institution, or their funder in advance of publication, rather than subscriptions paid by the reader or their institution after publication (Borrego, 2023). Most OA articles now published in journals recorded in databases such as Web of Science have involved payment of an APC, although most OA journals do not charge APCs (Morrison et al., 2022). Those not funded by APCs are generally sponsored by research funders or institutions. Still part of the broad 'gold' OA category, these OA journals not charging APCs have become known, somewhat confusingly, as 'diamond' OA journals (Becerril et al., 2021; Bosman et al., 2021). Diamond OA has often been favoured in LMICs, where OA implementations have typically been built on established approaches centred on non-commercial university presses.

The SciELO platform in Latin America, launched in 1998, is a prominent example of such an approach (Packer, 2020).

The APC model has also been adopted by publishers of established journals. Using the so-called 'hybrid' OA approach, they introduced charging of APCs for specific papers in subscription journals to make those papers OA from the middle of the first decade of the 21st century (Laakso & Björk, 2016). However, such an approach has proved controversial, since it ostensibly involves 'double dipping' by publishers – charging for both subscriptions and APCs for the same content (Asai, 2023; Mittermaier, 2015). One way of partly mitigating double dipping effects is to bundle up payments into so-called 'read-and-publish' agreements. Such agreements follow on from the practice established in the early 2000s of institutions (or consortia of institutions) paying journal subscriptions via 'big deals' – subscriptions paying for packages of online journals (Bergstrom et al., 2014). Read-and-publish deals have been designed to incorporate APCs into the big deal by enabling payment of APCs by institutions as annual block payments. Academic institutions pay *en bloc* for the APCs for a given year for articles published by authors within the institution (the 'publish' element) and that charge is then combined with the cost of subscriptions for other content supplied by the publisher (the 'read' element). Going further, some funders and institutions have come to insist that hybrid OA is completely phased out by ensuring read-and-publish deals become 'transformative' or 'transitional' agreements (Borrego et al., 2020). Transformative agreements represent attempts to convert subscription big deals into OA big deals by progressively phasing out the subscription ('read') payments and replacing them with block APC ('publish') payments only.

Of course, such models, like subscriptions before them, raise significant issues of affordability. Replacing subscriptions with APCs, even if managed as big deals or handled as block payments, has not resulted in overall cost savings for academic institutions, at least not so far, although access to content has been considerably expanded. Whilst arguably the APC business model changes the relationship between supplier and customer, making the publisher a provider of services contracted by research-performing institutions, that change does not yet seem to have resulted in the ability of customers to drive down prices through increased bargaining power. Even innovative models designed to leverage this bargaining power have had only limited success for the sector as a whole. SCOAP3 is an example: an innovative model in which consortia of institutions contract publishers to produce content for them following a procurement process (Kohls & Mele, 2018). This model appears to have potential but in practice has proved very difficult to set up because of the level of coordination required by the purchasing consortium. For the most part, prices charged for journals, whatever the charging model, remain stubbornly high (Puehringer et al., 2021). Commercial journal publishing continues to be a very profitable business. Costs are often beyond the reach of many researchers and their institutions in LMICs as well as HICs (high-income countries) – the basis of many criticisms of OA which I will discuss in this book.

It is the cost of scholarly journals, with the market dominated globally by a small number of large commercial journal publishers, with semi-oligopolistic power and profit margins to match (Larivière et al., 2015), that continues to give rise to calls for changes to the system. Sometimes, calls for change take the form of proposals to address specific inequities. For example, proposals such as differential pricing of APCs based on levels of country income, often involving waivers for countries with the lowest incomes, have been put forward (Estelle et al., 2023). The 'subscribe to open' business model, where library subscriptions are used to make publications openly available (assuming sufficient subscriptions can be raised), is sometimes seen as a pragmatic mode of flipping to OA (Crow et al., 2019). Diamond OA is seen by many as a more radical solution, often because it typically challenges the assumption of high-profit margins associated with commercial publishing (Dufour et al., 2023).

More radical solutions are also being discussed. The journal, it is argued, is basically a legacy publication model designed and priced for a print-based world. New, more efficient, and flexible approaches can now be developed in a digital environment, ones which take advantage of opportunities created by digital technologies. Many scholarly communication experiments and innovations are currently underway to test this, most of them with openness built in. They include new publishing platforms – which subvert the idea of the journal – and review services – which experiment with new forms of peer review. They often explicitly move away from commercialised publishing models. They aim still to deliver the main functions of scholarly communication – to disseminate quality-assured outputs of research as widely as possible in ways that can be cited and used by others – but do so in new ways, based on new business and funding models.

Across the different forms of OA, patterns of adoption still differ widely by discipline, institution, and country, among other variables (Huang et al., 2020; Moskovkin et al., 2021; Robinson-Garcia et al., 2020; Severin et al., 2020; Simard et al., 2022). Patterns of adoption have also varied by different output types, with OA books still being less mainstream mainly due to business models for OA monographs being less mature than for journals (Laakso, 2023). However, despite all these variations in adoption patterns, and the ongoing controversies about different implementation options, overall levels of OA are rising globally. In 2021, the providers of the Dimensions bibliographic database reported that for the first time in 2020, of the 6.6 million research outputs recorded that year, "more outputs were published through Open Access channels than traditional subscription channels globally" (Hook, 2021). A 2023 market report from the research data and analytics group, WordsRated, reported that 57% of the published literature was available in some form of OA, and that the market for OA in 2021 was worth $1.6 billion (Curcic, 2023). OA is fast becoming part of the mainstream for many, even if it is, at the same time, still associated with uncertainty and contestation.

With OA starting to become solidified in the practices of a growing number of scientists, even if it is still subject to widespread debate and variable patterns of uptake, it is a pressing challenge to ensure that OA works in a way that is both effective and equitable. By 'effective' I mean a system that successfully achieves the key functions of scholarly communication sustainably. By 'equitable' I mean a system which enables contributions from and facilitates usage by a diverse range of different actors in a way that is fair and does not disadvantage any individuals or groups. Both effectiveness and equity are important, and much of this book will involve exploring them further in relation to OA. It might be possible to argue that the distinction between effectiveness and equity is a false one – if the system is not equitable, it is not effective, for example. That may be true, but pragmatically, the two are often distinguished and we do know that the effectiveness of the science system can often be designed with only narrow interests in mind, creating a kind of effectiveness that is only for some. It is this issue that gives rise to the case I want to make in this book for scientific, epistemic, and participatory openness to help facilitate forms of global open access which are both effective and equitable. I will go on to discuss what these different forms of openness look like in relation to the outputs of research as the book progresses.

Open access does not exist in isolation, of course. When I refer to OA, I am referring to all aspects of openness that relate to scholarly communication (including journal publishing, preprinting, new publishing platforms, conference proceedings, and books and sections of books) but OA itself is one agenda in a wider set of open developments, collectively referred to as 'open science' or 'open research'. Open science (OS) includes a range of open practices, such as open data sharing, open peer review, and so on, alongside open access to research publications (Fecher & Friesike, 2014; Miedema, 2022; Vicente-Saez & Martinez-Fuentes, 2018). There are obvious points of connection between different forms of openness. Open access in scholarly communication and open data, for example, can be mutually supporting when sharing data can demonstrate the rigour of the research reported in the published paper and enable its reproducibility. Similarly, open peer review can work alongside OA, by making the process by which it achieves quality assurance for outputs transparent. These and other components of open science will, therefore, feature in this book. All of them are set in the wider research environment, of which openness is an increasingly important part, and it is essential to see OA in particular, and OS more generally, within that wider context of the global science system. My argument will, however, focus on OA, although, as I hope will become clear, much of the argument will also apply to different aspects of OS and will have implications for the wider research environment.

Overview of this book

In this book I will explore the current debates on global OA, engaging with relevant theory and current practice. Having sketched out some of the background in this chapter, I will go on in Chapter 2 to outline the key arguments historically made to support OA. I will then set out criticisms that have been levelled at global aspects of OA in recent years, both theoretical and practical criticisms. OA has been seen as imposing exploitative business and publishing models on low- and middle-income countries, and creating, perpetuating, or exacerbating exclusionary research systems and cultures. It has also been seen as a vehicle for oppression and epistemic injustice. In Chapter 2, I will discuss these criticisms, defining some of the key concepts in the process, including epistemic injustice. The chapter, therefore, sets out the central dilemma that the rest of the book aims to explore.

In Chapter 3, I will go on to show how the case made for scientific openness has often been based on normative and universalistic views of science derived from positivist or adapted-positivist meta-theory. This introduces us to one of the key issues with which this book engages: much of the debate about OA is actually about knowledge itself – about what constitutes valid and valuable knowledge. The case for openness presumes that the outputs of science are universally valid and valuable, at least in some sense, otherwise they would not be worth sharing. Openness in science is often justified as a means of improving the effectiveness and efficiency of the research system. The use of arguments like transparency and accountability, mean openness in science can also be seen within a frame of liberal social theory, and within that frame, as a form of distributive epistemic justice. These arguments are important but, I will suggest, they only get us so far. In fact, they highlight important questions that still need to be addressed.

In Chapter 4, I will outline some of the problems with the (adapted-) positivist perspective which points us in the direction of more construc- tionist paradigms, widening our perspective on valid and valuable knowledge, and accommodating various epistemic systems. This is the basis of what I call, epistemic openness. I will argue for a broad understanding of 'science' to cover the range of academic disciplines, but also argue for the further expansion of ideas of valid and valuable knowledge to extend to other knowledge systems. I will outline how an interaction between science and other epistemic systems can be approached and I will highlight some of the questions arising from such exchanges.

Nevertheless, many constructionist accounts, some using critical and postcolonial theory, also see knowledge as a means of epistemic or cognitive oppression, something on which I will focus in Chapter 5. I will explore 'softer' and 'harder' versions of the idea of epistemic or cognitive oppression. Softer forms relate to problems such as bias, a major challenge which needs to be addressed in its many forms in science. Harder forms of the idea of epistemic oppression see knowledge as a vehicle for hegemonic power. I will investigate some of the bases for this idea. I will argue this position is based on a thoroughgoing construc- tionist foundation which results in problems of relativism and incommensurability of knowledges. It also does not provide grounding for any kind of ethical position supportive of OA. In fact, it ultimately undermines the case for OA: why widely share information and knowledge that is oppressive?

In Chapter 6, I will look in some detail at the idea of the "ecologies of knowledges" put forward by Santos and others. This idea appears to offer some hope in addressing the problems of relativism and incommensurability. The ecologies of knowledges concept is useful in that it gives us a clear view of global inequities associated with knowledge and a rich understanding of the potential of interactions across epistemic boundaries. However, I will argue, the ecologies of knowledges idea still does not eliminate the problems of relativism and incommensurability.

I will go on, in Chapter 7, to propose that an approach underpinned by critical realism can help address these problems. A type of realism accommodating a "moderate constructionism" (Elder-Vass, 2012), critical realism steers a course between positivist and anti-positivist meta-theory, and is conducive to OA, since it encourages a multi-faceted view of reality and ongoing discussion and debate about it. A critical realist position recognises the importance of judgemental rationality, enabling incommensurable arguments to be evaluated in relation to each other. Furthermore, it can form the basis of an ethically informed emancipatory case for an equitable global openness, and one that uses openness as a means to begin to address epistemic biases and injustices.

After this more elaborate discussion of epistemic openness and its limits, I will then move on, in Chapter 8, to explore some of the dimensions of participatory openness. I will discuss aspects of culture and economics important in enabling people from different contexts and regions to contribute to science and engage in the interchange between science and other knowledge systems. I will argue that doing so is important in addressing existing participatory injustices.

In Chapter 9, I will draw these different strands together. I will summarise the case for scientific, epistemic, and participatory openness, which I believe need to be meaningfully combined to create a global open access environment which is effective and equitable.

My argument in the book as a whole will involve working on different levels of abstraction and practicality, of theory and practice. The foundational level I will discuss concerns the meta-theoretical assumptions that underpin perspectives on OA – how we understand reality and our knowledge of it, and what this means for OA. I will also cover social theory, which is based on meta-theory, and which is designed to help us explain major social and cultural developments, including OA. In addition, I will spend some time discussing the philosophical idea of epistemic injustice and its relationship with social theory. Furthermore, I will consider issues at a very practical level, exploring questions which arise from and feed into theory – ideas of business and sustainability models for OA, governance and policy approaches to openness, and technologies and processes that support open science. Wherever possible, I will try to show links between these levels – in fact doing so will be crucial, since, as I have mentioned, many of the disputes we see about issues of OA policy and practice in fact stem from fundamental theoretical disagreements.

Inevitably, my approach will be a broad-brush one. I will be drawing on a range of literatures, intentionally, as the issues involved benefit from broad cross-disciplinary insights. However, I recognise this runs the risk of dealing with things in a rather crude way. I will engage with a range of theories, but focus on the ways they relate to OA. I realise this does create the danger of my treatment of them being rather one-dimensional. I will be jumping into the middle of some long-standing debates in a variety of areas because of their relationship with openness. I know this creates risks, not least of failing to convey context and nuance in my treatment of those disparate areas. I cannot deal with everything at the level of detail I would like, but I hope I can do enough at least to establish a credible case and construct a useful framework suggestive of further research and action.

This book has been written to contribute to the OA literature and to inform OA practice. It has therefore been framed in a way that I hope is approachable to those involved in the practice of OA as well as those interested in theory. With that in mind, I have deliberately unpacked certain ideas, aiming to enhance clarity. I am hoping to strike a balance between, on the one hand, providing a succinct statement of the key arguments, whilst on the other hand, elaborating the arguments sufficiently to provide an evidenced and coherent case. In that way, I hope this book will make a positive contribution to the work of a wide range of researchers, policymakers, and practitioners as we work towards achieving a more effective and equitable global open access environment.

References

Asai, S. (2023). Does double dipping occur? The case of Wiley's hybrid journals. *Scientometrics*. 10.1007/s11192-023-04800-8

Bashir, S., Gul, S., Bashir, S., Nisa, N. T., & Ganaie, S. A. (2021). Evolution of institutional repositories: Managing institutional research output to remove the gap of academic elitism. *Journal of Librarianship and Information Science, 54*(3), 518–531. 10.1177/09610006211009592

Becerril, A., Bosman, J., Bjørnshauge, L., Frantsvåg, J. E., Kramer, B., Langlais, P.-C., Mounier, P., Proudman, V., Redhead, C., & Torny, D. (2021). *OA Diamond Journals Study. Part 2: Recommendations*. Zenodo. 10.5281/zenodo.4562790

Bergstrom, T. C., Courant, P. N., Mcafee, R. P., & Williams, M. A. (2014). Evaluating big deal journal bundles. *Proceedings of the National Academy of Sciences, 111*(26), 9425–9430. 10.1073/pnas.1403006111

Borrego, Á. (2023). Article processing charges for open access journal publishing: A review. *Learned Publishing, 36*(3), 359–378. 10.1002/leap.1558

Borrego, Á., Anglada, L., & Abadal, E. (2020). Transformative agreements: Do they pave the way to open access? *Learned Publishing, 34*(2), 216–232. 10.1002/leap.1347

Bosman, J., Frantsvåg, J. E., Kramer, B., Langlais, P.-C., & Proudman, V. (2021). *OA Diamond Journals Study. Part 1: Findings*. Zenodo. 10.5281/zenodo.4558704

Chiarelli, A., Johnson, R., Pinfield, S., & Richens, E. (2019). Preprints and scholarly communication: An exploratory qualitative study of adoption, practices, drivers and barriers. *F1000Research, 8*. 10.12688/f1000research.19619.2

Connelly, B. S., Ones, D. S., & Chernyshenko, O. S. (2014). Introducing the special section on openness to experience: Review of openness taxonomies, measurement, and nomological net. *Journal of Personality Assessment, 96*(1), 1–16. 10.1080/00223891.2013.830620

Crow, R., Gallagher, R., & Naim, K. (2019). Subscribe to open: A practical approach for converting subscription journals to open access. *Learned Publishing, 33*(2), 181–185. 10.1002/leap.1262

Curcic, D. (2023, June 2). Open access publishing statistics. *WordsRated*. https://wordsrated.com/open-access-publishing-statistics/

Drake, T., Gulliver, S., & Harle, J. (2023). *Research publishing is an under-recognised global challenge: Opportunities for the G20 to act (306; CGD Policy Paper)*. Center for Global Development. https://www.cgdev.org/publication/research-publishing-under-recognised-global-challenge-opportunities-g20-act

Dufour, Q., Pontille, D., & Torny, D. (2023). *Supporting diamond open access journals. Interest and feasibility of direct funding mechanisms*. bioRxiv. 10.1101/2023.05.03.539231

Elder-Vass, D. (2012). *The reality of social construction*. Cambridge University Press.

Estelle, L., Jago, D., Mentink, H., & Wise, A. (2023). *Developing a globally fair pricing model for academic publishing*. Information Power commissioned by cOAlition S. https://www.coalition-s.org/wp-content/uploads/2023/09/Fairer PricingFrameworkConsultation_15Sept2023.pdf

Fecher, B., & Friesike, S. (2014). Open science: One term, five schools of thought. In S. Bartling & S. Friesike (Eds.), *Opening science: The evolving guide on how the internet is changing research, collaboration and scholarly publishing* (pp. 17–47). Springer. 10.1007/978-3-319-00026-8_2

Hillard, T., & Baber, R. (2021). Peer review: The cornerstone of scientific publishing integrity. *Climacteric*, *24*(2), 107–108. 10.1080/13697137.2021.1882140

Hook, D. (2021, February 24). Open access surpasses subscription publication globally for the first time. *Dimensions*. https://www.dimensions.ai/blog/open-access-surpasses-subscription-publication-globally-for-the-first-time/

Huang, C.-K., Neylon, C., Hosking, R., Montgomery, L., Wilson, K. S., Ozaygen, A., & Brookes-Kenworthy, C. (2020). Evaluating the impact of open access policies on research institutions. *eLife*, *9*, e57067. 10.7554/eLife.57067

Ingrams, A. (2020). Administrative reform and the quest for openness: A Popperian review of open government. *Administration & Society*, *52*(2), 319–340. 10.1177/0095399719875460

Knöchelmann, M. (2021). The democratisation myth: Open access and the solidification of epistemic injustices. *Science & Technology Studies*, *34*(2), Article 2. 10.23987/sts.94964

Kohls, A., & Mele, S. (2018). Converting the literature of a scientific field to open access through global collaboration: The experience of SCOAP3 in particle physics. *Publications*, *6*(2), 15–15. 10.3390/publications6020015

Laakso, M. (2023). Open access books through open data sources: Assessing prevalence, providers, and preservation. *Journal of Documentation*, *79*(7), 157–177. 10.1108/JD-02-2023-0016

Laakso, M., & Björk, B.-C. (2016). Hybrid open access—A longitudinal study. *Journal of Informetrics*, *10*(4), 919–932. 10.1016/j.joi.2016.08.002

Larivière, V., Haustein, S., & Mongeon, P. (2015). The oligopoly of academic publishers in the digital era. *PLoS One*, *10*(6), e0127502. 10.1371/journal.pone.0127502

Larivière, V., & Sugimoto, C. R. (2018). Do authors comply when funders enforce open access to research? *Nature*, *562*(7728), 483–486. 10.1038/d41586-018-07101-w

Mboa Nkoudou, T. H. (2020). Epistemic alienation in African scholarly communications: Open access as a pharmakon. In M. P. Eve & J. Gray (Eds.), *Reassembling scholarly communications: Histories, infrastructures, and global politics of open access*. MIT Press. 10.7551/mitpress/11885.003.0006

Miedema, F. (2022). *Open science: The very idea*. Springer Netherlands. 10.1007/978-94-024-2115-6

Mittermaier, B. (2015). Double dipping in hybrid open access – Chimera or reality? *ScienceOpen Research*. 10.14293/S2199-1006.1.SOR-SOCSCI.AOWNTU.v1

Montalbano, P. (2011). Trade openness and developing countries' vulnerability: Concepts, misconceptions, and directions for research. *World Development*, *39*(9), 1489–1502. 10.1016/j.worlddev.2011.02.009

Moore, S. (2017). A genealogy of open access: Negotiations between openness and access to research. *Revue Française Des Sciences de l'information et de La Communication*, *11*. 10.4000/rfsic.3220

Moore, S. (2019). *Revisiting 'the 1990s debutante': Scholar-led publishing and the pre-history of the open access movement.* 10.17613/gty2-w177

Morrison, H., Borges, L., Zhao, X., Kakou, T. L., & Shanbhoug, A. N. (2022). Change and growth in open access journal publishing and charging trends 2011–2021. *Journal of the Association for Information Science and Technology, 73*(12), 1793–1805. 10.1002/asi.24717

Moskovkin, V. M., Saprykina, T. V., Sadovski, M. V., & Serkina, O. V. (2021). International movement of open access to scientific knowledge: A quantitative analysis of country involvement. *Journal of Academic Librarianship, 47*(1), 102296. 10.1016/j.acalib.2020.102296

Mulligan, A., Hall, L., & Raphael, E. (2013). Peer review in a changing world: An international study measuring the attitudes of researchers. *Journal of the American Society for Information Science and Technology, 64*(1), 132–161. 10.1002/asi.22798

Nicholas, D., Watkinson, A., Jamali, H. R., Herman, E., Tenopir, C., Volentine, R., Allard, S., & Levine, K. (2015). Peer review: Still king in the digital age. *Learned Publishing, 28*(1), 15–21. 10.1087/20150104

Ola, K. (2018). *Open access to knowledge in Nigeria: A framework for developing countries.* Routledge. 10.4324/9780429446795

Packer, A. (2020). The pasts, presents, and futures of SciELO. In M. P. Eve & J. Gray (Eds.), *Reassembling scholarly communications: Histories, infrastructures, and global politics of open access* (pp. 297–313). MIT Press. 10.7551/mitpress/11885.003.0030

Piron, F. (2018). Postcolonial open access. In U. Herb & J. Schopfel (Eds.), *Open divide: Critical studies in open access.* Litwin Books. http://hdl.handle.net/20.500.11794/16178

Puehringer, S., Rath, J., & Griesebner, T. (2021). The political economy of academic publishing: On the commodification of a public good. *PLoS One, 16*(6), e0253226. 10.1371/journal.pone.0253226

Robinson-Garcia, N., Costas, R., & van Leeuwen, T. N. (2020). Open access uptake by universities worldwide. *PeerJ, 8*, e9410. 10.7717/peerj.9410

Sengupta, P. (2021). Open access publication: Academic colonialism or knowledge philanthropy? *Geoforum, 118*(1), 203–206. 10.1016/j.geoforum.2020.04.001

Severin, A., Egger, M., Eve, M. P., & Hürlimann, D. (2020). Discipline-specific open access publishing practices and barriers to change: An evidence-based review. *F1000Research, 7*, 1925. 10.12688/f1000research.17328.2

Simard, M.-A., Ghiasi, G., Mongeon, P., & Larivière, V. (2022). National differences in dissemination and use of open access literature. *PLoS One, 17*(8), e0272730. 10.1371/journal.pone.0272730

Smith, R. (2006). Peer review: A flawed process at the heart of science and journals. *Journal of the Royal Society of Medicine, 99*(4), 178–182. 10.1177/014107680609900414

Suber, P. (2012). *Open access.* MIT Press. http://mitpress.mit.edu/books/open-access

Vicente-Saez, R., & Martinez-Fuentes, C. (2018). Open science now: A systematic literature review for an integrated definition. *Journal of Business Research, 88*, 428–436. 10.1016/J.JBUSRES.2017.12.043

Waltman, L., Kaltenbrunner, W., Pinfield, S., & Woods, H. B. (2022). *How to improve scientific peer review: Four schools of thought.* SocArXiv. 10.31235/osf.io/v8ghj

Willinsky, J. (2006). *The access principle: The case for open access to research and scholarship.* MIT Press.

2 Critique of global open access

In this chapter, I want to begin by briefly reviewing the case commonly made for the benefits of global open access, using one of its formative statements, the Budapest Open Access Initiative declaration, as a starting point. I will then outline how OA has been critiqued, including through the lens of critical and postcolonial theory. In this chapter, I will focus primarily on work that engages with OA specifically and provide an initial overview of the key arguments involved. Later in the book (Chapters 4–6), I will expand on the analysis and explore in more detail some of the theories on which critics of OA have built their arguments. Focusing on OA and the way it has been critiqued at this stage will help to define and clarify the central dilemma the rest of the book goes on to discuss.

Open access advocacy

Advocates of open access have often included amongst their stated aims improving access to research outputs on a global basis. That includes access for users within academic institutions and beyond the academy, within low- and middle-income countries (LMICs), as well as those in high-income countries (HICs). OA, it is claimed, will enhance the research process itself, by ensuring all those in the research community can access and make use of all the available literature in a timely way, including those in LMICs, where there have always been major access problems (Boudry et al., 2019). Scientific progress is partly achieved through communication, enabling new research to build on previous work. Making the results of research available as widely as possible through open access, it is argued, enables the global science system to work more effectively (Pinfield et al., 2020).

At the same time, it is suggested that open access also produces wider societal benefits. Areas ranging from health care to economic development are seen as potentially benefiting worldwide from OA (ElSabry, 2017), particularly when combined with initiatives to promote use of the

DOI: 10.4324/9781032679259-2

scholarly literature beyond the academy (Elliott & Resnik, 2019). Cockerill and Knols (2008), observe that:

> *In combination with appropriate local skills and expertise, online access to the latest research can help low-income countries not only deal with practical priorities in areas such as public health and agriculture but also provide a vital starting point to developing their own research capacity.*
>
> (Cockerill & Knols, 2008, p. 66)

Open access, it is argued, can enhance the scientific capacity of LMICs, promote collaborative working with HICs, and create societal benefits in areas such as health care and agricultural development.

The Budapest Open Access Initiative (BOAI) statement, often seen as a touchstone for the principles underpinning OA, states the case for open access to the research literature in idealistic terms:

> *Removing access barriers to this literature will accelerate research, enrich education, share the learning of the rich with the poor and the poor with the rich, make this literature as useful as it can be, and lay the foundation for uniting humanity in a common intellectual conversation and quest for knowledge.*
>
> (BOAI, 2002)

The reciprocity in this definition is often implicit in the case made for OA: widening the pool of contributors to the scholarly communication system, not just consumers of content, resulting in mutual benefits. Whilst the drivers for opening up research may often be framed in instrumental terms (such as improving the efficiency and effectiveness of scholarly communication), other more fundamental motivations, such as those in the BOAI declaration, are sometimes expressed. Discussing people involved in open research, a report from the Open Scholarship Initiative in 2020 stated, "the people in this community share a common motive—idealism—to make research better able to serve the public good" (Hampson, 2020, p. 5). The language of 'public good' has often accompanied OA advocacy.

Potential societal benefits of open access are sometimes linked with the idea of OA as an ethical imperative, an idea that has been present in discussions on OA throughout its history. Bacevic and Muellerleile (2018) build a case for OA as a "moral good", arguing that knowledge is a public good that has the potential to "do good", yielding benefits "connected to democracy and equality, and to dismantling hierarchies – including those, such as that between North and South" (p. 183). Therefore, those who produce and "help others to access" knowledge are performing a positive "moral" role. Fowler (2014), as a journal editor working in the field of ethnobiology, expresses the view that OA is "moral" in practical terms:

> *Open access is moral primarily, I believe, since it places high quality scholarly information into anyone's hands at no cost and from any location where the Internet is available.*
>
> (Fowler, 2014, p. 1)

In this way, Fowler regards OA as contributing to "social justice". Others have made the case for OA in terms of social justice, either in general terms (Scherlen & Robinson, 2008), or specifically in relation to LMICs (Arunachalam, 2017). Yamey (2008) argued that open access to biomedical literature is a human rights issue, and lack of access is "a rights violation that impedes global health". Ahmed (2007) argued that open access is one important means of addressing Africa's "scientific information famine".

Because of the apparent benefits of open access, many governments and other funders of research have adopted policies encouraging or even mandating holders of their grants or institutions they fund to make their outputs open access (Mering, 2020). Open access in particular, and open science more generally, are increasingly seen as a necessary part of "a well-functioning science system" (Science Europe, 2022). Organisations, such as development charities, including INASP (International Network for Advancing Science and Policy), and intergovernmental organisations, such as the OECD, have adopted positive positions in relation to OA as furthering international development objectives (Gwynn, 2019). In a report published by INASP for the UK's Foreign, Commonwealth and Development Office, Harle and Warne (2019) mapped out in detail the policy actions needed to ensure that those in LMICs can benefit from OA. Following the coronavirus pandemic, in which OA and OS were seen as accelerating the response to the global emergency (Kadakia et al., 2021), some studies have made the case that OA and OS can help address other global challenges, such as the international strategic development goals (SDGs) (Havemann et al., 2020; Okafor et al., 2022).

Over the last two decades, calls to accelerate open science developments in general, and open access in particular, have often been made by researchers and organisations from LMICs (Havemann et al., 2020; Okafor et al., 2022). The case has been made in terms of the potential benefits that open access to research outputs and data are likely to bring to LIMICs, for example, in terms of medicine and health (Anagnostou et al., 2019). Studies of various LMICs have shown increasing adoption of open practices (Minniti et al., 2018; Mwangi et al., 2021). Policies and infrastructures to support OA have been developed and improved progressively in LMICs, although there is still some way to go in making OA work effectively.

Criticisms of global open access

However, in recent years, OA has been subjected to increasing criticism. Instead of a means of achieving public good, OA has been characterised as a vehicle for hegemonic power, allowing dominant groups to exercise power over others – in particular, actors in the Global North exercising exploitative power over the Global South (Knöchelmann, 2021; Piron, 2018; Sengupta, 2021). This sort of criticism is not new – Haider (2007) outlined many of its key elements in 2007. Taking as her starting point the BOAI statement and its reference to "the rich and the poor" and "other curious minds", Haider argued that the BOAI failed to take into account power asymmetries, which limited the positive impact of OA. Such criticism has gained momentum in the last decade. Often informed by critical and postcolonial theory, these accounts portray OA as an instrument of knowledge-based hegemonic power, an aspect of neo-colonialism which generates epistemic or cognitive injustices: where Western knowledge systems, such as science produced in the Western tradition, dominate and marginalise indigenous knowledges.

The critique of OA, broadly speaking, takes three related forms:

- Critique 1: OA is observed to impose inappropriate and unsustainable business and publishing models on researchers from low-resource regions and their institutions, with the system dominated by large corporations based in Western Europe and North America.
- Critique 2: OA is also portrayed as perpetuating or exacerbating inequities inherent in the scholarly communication system, research evaluation system, and the academy in general, limiting the participation of people in LMICs.
- Critique 3: OA is seen by some critics as a way of dominating LMICs with alien and oppressive forms of knowledge associated with the Global North, devaluing indigenous knowledge forms, and creating epistemic injustice.

The first two of these critiques concern participatory barriers, observed to have been created or perpetuated by OA, despite the claims of its advocates that it lowers them. In critique 1, the business model of article-processing charges (APCs) has been the subject of particular criticism (Cox, 2023; Kwon, 2022; Mboa Nkoudou, 2020; Piron, 2018; Rodrigues et al., 2022). APCs are seen as unaffordable for many people in LMICs, with the system pricing them out of contributing to the scholarly literature. More recently, 'read-and-publish' agreements (where institutions pay annual fees which combine subscription and publication charges) have similarly been criticised as unaffordable for institutions in LMICs (Raju et al., 2020).

At the same time, critique 2 above has focused on barriers to participation created by Western, English-language-biased systems of prestige and reward (Piron et al., 2021). Researchers in LMICs experience pressure to participate in a 'recognition' or 'reputation' economy (Fecher et al., 2017; Pinfield et al., 2020) that is governed and resourced in favour of Western researchers. This includes pressure to publish in particular journals, such as those indexed in the Web of Science (WoS), where inclusion in WoS is regarded as a mark of quality. The journal metric assigned by WoS calculating the average number of times articles in a particular journal are cited – the impact factor – is especially used as a proxy of the quality of articles (Archambault & Larivière, 2009). Publication in journals with high journal impact factors is seen as important for status and career progression, even though these journals are mostly published by Western publishers, governed by editorial boards made up of members predominantly from the HICs, and edited by researchers usually from large, well-resourced Western institutions. Many authors from non-Anglophone LMICs face additional barriers of language in participating in the scientific discourse (Bahji et al., 2023), something Clavero (2010) calls "linguistic injustice".

Critique 3 pushes the criticism of OA beyond that of business models, academic cultures, and languages to focus on knowledge itself, using concepts like cognitive or epistemic injustice. The term, "cognitive injustice", is used by Piron to mean, "anything that can prevent researchers from deploying the full potential of their research capacities in the service of sustainable local development" (Piron, 2018, p. 119). The term "epistemic injustice" can also be used in this generalised way. However, "epistemic injustice" can in addition be used more precisely, based on the conceptualisation of epistemic injustice advanced by Miranda Fricker (2007) and others. Fricker (2007) defines epistemic injustice as "a wrong done to someone specifically in their capacity as a knower", and in her early work she focuses on two major types of epistemic injustice: "testimonial injustice" and "hermeneutical injustice". "Testimonial injustice", Fricker states, "occurs when prejudice causes a hearer to give a deflated level of credibility to a speaker's word" (p. 1). Someone's word is doubted or disbelieved in an unfair discriminatory way, often based on their identity or perceived identity. "Hermeneutical injustice occurs at a prior stage, when a gap in collective interpretive resources puts someone at an unfair disadvantage when it comes to making sense of their social experiences" (p. 1). Someone working with a different set of cultural assumptions, for example, might be unfairly seen as less intelligent. Testimonial injustice is an injustice associated with the subject's "credibility" – they experience deflated credibility – and hermeneutical injustice is an injustice associated with the subject's "intelligibility" – they experience deflated intelligibility (Fricker, 2007, 2013).

Knöchelmann's (2021) critique of OA applies these types of epistemic injustice to scholarly communication. He argues that testimonial injustice occurs when scholars from the Global South are "preemptively silenced" by practices such as peer review, which are biased against them. Cox (2023) makes a similar point about APCs, regarding them as a vehicle of testimonial injustice, since "the APC publishing model systematically excludes researchers from the Global South on non-meritocratic grounds" (Cox, 2023, p. 520). Knöchelmann goes on to argue that the low contribution of scholarship from the Global South to the international scholarly literature, especially research using the "hermeneutical resources" and knowledge systems of the Global South, is evidence of hermeneutical injustice. Knöchelmann also suggests that "epistemic objectification" is evident in scholarly communication. Fricker (2007) defines "epistemic objectification" as a consequence of testimonial injustice, at the more severe end, which "demotes the speaker from informant to source of information, from subject to object" (p. 133). This can occur in research where peoples from the Global South become the objects of research, rather than participants, denying their "epistemic agency" (Dotson, 2014), and separating them from any benefits of the research. Knöchelmann provides examples of where this has happened in a wide range of research disciplines and argues it is another form of epistemic injustice amplified by OA.

Other forms of epistemic injustice have been defined in the literature, some of which may apply to scholarly communication. Hookway (2010) identifies a wider set of epistemic injustices relating to testimonial injustice that "can prevent someone from participating in inquiry" – a kind of 'participatory injustice'. This applies to the opportunity and capacity to make a meaningful contribution and is potentially a wider category than testimonial or hermeneutical injustice but still has important epistemic dimensions. In an academic setting, it could relate to the constraints experienced by researchers in LMICs to contribute to scholarly interactions in framing questions, presenting ideas, and engaging in debate. This is similar to Dotson's (2012) idea of "contributory exclusion"; Dotson uses the term "exclusion" to emphasise the effect of the actions involved.

Since her early work defining what she came to call "discriminatory epistemic injustice" (testimonial and hermeneutical epistemic injustice), Fricker has elaborated the concept, discussing another strand of epistemic injustice, "distributive epistemic injustice" (Fricker, 2013). She defines the latter as, "the unfair distribution of epistemic goods such as education or information" (Fricker, 2013, p. 1318). Fricker observes that this kind of epistemic injustice fits more obviously with liberal notions of justice, but, because it is a more apparent injustice, it has not to date been the focus of her own work. Coady (2010, 2017) has proposed that all forms of epistemic injustice are in fact distributive in nature. However, Fricker (2017) has pushed back on this and reasserted the discriminatory/distributive distinction. Although important in contributing to our thinking on open access, as we shall see later, the concept of distributive epistemic injustice has received less attention in OA discussions compared with that of discriminatory epistemic injustice. It does, however, seem to have the potential to help us understand some of the benefits of OA.

Critical and postcolonial theory and OA

Many of the contributions to the debate about OA draw on critical and postcolonial theories. For example, theories of hegemony, whose antecedence can be traced back to Gramsci (1937) are evident in discussion of the academic power of the Global North. Knöchelmann (2021) uses the concept of "hegemony" to explain the dominance of the North in scholarly communication reinforced by OA, which he characterises as "hegemonic openness". He goes on to explain how he sees this working, through scientific knowledge and social systems, which he summarises using the Foucauldian ideas of "discourses" – ways of seeing and talking about the world which establish and reinforce social and behavioural norms (Foucault, 1972) – and "epistemes" – frameworks of thought and cultural assumptions that underpin social systems (Foucault, 1971):

> *Hegemony is reinforced by the impact of largescale OA. The journal as a "white epistemic institution" (Pohlhaus, 2017: 15) as well as the established book publishing venues keep their structural dominance by manifesting existing power structures in scholarly communication. They keep being governed by scholars of the Global North and their epistemes. Instead of an opening up of discourses—a globalisation in form [sic] of a global inclusion—the Global North governance causes an expansion of discourses to be an expansion of the dominance of the Global North that either excludes epistemes or demands the adjustment of other social groups to Western norms. Such an expansion is unreflective of the situatedness of knowledge in that it leads to epistemic adjustments to the norms of existing discourse practices of the Global North. Understanding and meaning, thus, loose [sic] parts of their specificity and contextual relevance for the community it was produced in and, originally, for.*
>
> (Knöchelmann, 2021, p. 78)

Open access, working through conventional publishing channels (such as books and journals) and produced by established publishers, is a vehicle for "an expansion of the dominance of the Global North" over the Global South by enabling the discourses and epistemes of the Global North to be imposed on the Global South. Significantly, in this critique, knowledge (and it is scientific knowledge we are talking about) is characterised by "situatedness", and knowledge generated in and for the Global North comes to dominate that of the Global South. Open access makes this knowledge from the Global North more widely available, promoting the "dominance of the Global North".

Such critiques of OA have become more prominent during the second decade of the 21st century (see for example collections in Eve & Gray, 2020; Meagher, 2021). They often use language, characteristic of postcolonial narratives: the Global North/Global South dichotomy sustained through discourses and power structures which perpetuate Global North dominance and impose on communities in the Global South forms of knowledge which are alien to them. The language is often very strong. For example, summarising the direction taken by OA in the first 20 years of the 21st century, Mboa Nkoudou (2020) says that OA, at least in its current form,

has had disastrous consequences in the African academic milieu. Amongst them is epistemic alienation, symptomatized by epistemicides (killing of indigenous people's knowledge), and linguicides (killing of indigenous people's languages). It is true that epistemicides and linguicides preexisted OA; but the way OA is going at the global level, and the lack of awareness at the local level, reinforces and accentuates these preexisting problems. On this basis, open access currently contains within it the germs of epistemic poison for Africa.

(Mboa Nkoudou, 2020, p. 34)

Because it has made knowledge generated outside Africa more readily available, OA has had the effect of "killing" indigenous knowledges and languages, or at least strengthening those pre-existing trends. OA is important in that it amplifies knowledge from the Global North making it difficult for other voices to be heard. This is not just an argument about business models or academic cultures, but an argument about knowledge itself.

We will go on to consider these arguments in detail later, but what will be immediately clear is just how challenging they are for OA advocates. OA advocates have often assumed openness to be a self-evident good for the global scientific community and potentially beneficial for wider society (including people in LMICs). However, now OA looks tainted. It is pictured as exclusionary and inequitable. It is seen as a vehicle for "dominance", or even as a "poison", which has had the effect of "killing" the knowledges and languages of indigenous peoples in LMICs. Far from being a "moral" development inspired by "idealism", OA is seen as problematic, even unethical.

All three critiques of OA I have described are interrelated. APC-based or other high-cost business models (critique 1) may often support a system of prestige based on high-impact-factor journals (critique 2). Adoption of such markers of esteem by institutions in LMICs (critique 2) may in turn cause scholars there to focus their work within particular epistemic systems and neglect other forms of knowledge (critique 3). Exclusionary business models (critique 1) and inequitable reward structures (critique 2) act as enablers of epistemic injustice, limiting the participation of certain actors and pushing them to work in ways not suited to their own context or interests (critique 3).

However, critiques 1–3 remain conceptually distinct and have different practical implications. It is one thing to argue that certain modes of open access have created or perpetuated inequities (critique 1) or that incentive and reward structures and academic cultures are exclusionary (critique 2), but it is another thing to state that the knowledge being made available in an OA form is in itself a vehicle of neo-colonial oppression (critique 3). Critiques 1 and 2 can be addressed by developing business models, policies, infrastructures, systems, and cultures in such a way as to minimise inequities, however difficult that may be in practice. In contrast, critique 3 cannot be addressed so easily (either conceptually or practically), since it calls into question our whole understanding of what constitutes valid and valuable knowledge embodied in scholarly literature.

Despite the criticisms, it is noteworthy that OA advocacy and policy development, on the one hand, and critique of OA, on the other hand, have often continued along parallel tracks, with limited interaction, particularly around the critique of epistemic issues. There has been some discussion on business models and incentive systems in the peer-reviewed and professional literature relating to OA, but serious engagement with epistemic questions is much rarer. Although there are exceptions (Chan et al., 2020), most often, advocates and critics of OA have simply talked past each other, using different conceptual frames and terminologies.

It is this situation I would like to try to address in this book by bringing advocacy and critique of OA into conversation with each other. All the criticisms are intertwined, and so it is important to consider them all, but in doing so, I want to give the most attention to the critique of OA as epistemic injustice and oppression (critique 3) – the issue is so foundational and yet comparatively little discussed. My argument will be that, between them, scientific, epistemic, and participatory openness can make a substantial contribution to addressing all three critiques and mitigating the challenges that they identify. That is not to say, of course, these things are somehow easy – quite the opposite. Part of what I will argue is just how difficult these challenges are and how addressing them requires change at every conceivable level. This can only begin, however, when we bring the key ideas into meaningful conversation with one another, and we start to understand the complexity of the issues. Without losing sight of its benefits, we need to see beyond the narrow view that more OA will be sufficient to solve all the major problems.

In order to bring the arguments of advocates of OA and its critics into conversation with one another, we need to explore how the case for open access has developed and what theoretical presumptions underlie the case (which are typically left unacknowledged). When we understand the theoretical and practical grounds on which the case for OA has been built, we will be better positioned to understand how those grounds have been challenged. Only then can a meaningful conversation begin and some sort of resolution (even if tentative) developed. We will take a first step in this direction in the next chapter by thinking about some of the key assumptions that underpin the case for scientific openness as it has often been made.

References

Ahmed, A. (2007). Open access towards bridging the digital divide: Policies and strategies for developing countries. *Information Technology for Development, 13*(4), 337–361. 10.1002/itdj.20067

Anagnostou, A., Taylor, S. J. E., Groen, D., Suleimenova, D., Anokye, N., Bruno, R., & Barbera, R. (2019). Building global research capacity in public health: The case of a science gateway for physical activity lifelong modelling and simulation. *2019 Winter Simulation Conference (WSC)*, 1067–1078. 10.11 09/WSC40007.2019.9004845

Archambault, É., & Larivière, V. (2009). History of the journal impact factor: Contingencies and consequences. *Scientometrics, 79*(3), 635–649. 10.1007/s111 92-007-2036-x

Arunachalam, S. (2017). Social justice in scholarly publishing: Open access is the only way. *The American Journal of Bioethics, 17*(10), 15–17. 10.1080/15265161. 2017.1366194

Bacevic, J., & Muellerleile, C. (2018). The moral economy of open access. *European Journal of Social Theory, 21*(2), 169–188. 10.1177/1368431017717368

Bahji, A., Acion, L., Laslett, A.-M., & Adinoff, B. (2023). Exclusion of the non-English-speaking world from the scientific literature: Recommendations for change for addiction journals and publishers. *Nordic Studies on Alcohol and Drugs, 40*(1), 6–13. 10.1177/14550725221102227

BOAI. (2002). *Budapest open access initiative.* http://www.budapestopenaccessinitiative. org/read

Boudry, C., Alvarez-Muñoz, P., Arencibia-Jorge, R., Ayena, D., Brouwer, N. J., Chaudhuri, Z., Chawner, B., Epee, E., Erraïs, K., Fotouhi, A., Gharaibeh, A. M., Hassanein, D. H., Herwig-Carl, M. C., Howard, K., Kaimbo, D. K. W., Laughrea, P.-A., Lopez, F. A., Machin-Mastromatteo, J. D., Malerbi, F. K., ..., Mouriaux, F. (2019). Worldwide inequality in access to full text scientific articles: The example of ophthalmology. *PeerJ, 7*, e7850. 10.7717/peerj.7850

Chan, L., Hall, B., Piron, F., Tandon, R., & Williams, L. (2020). *Open science beyond open access: For and with communities: A step towards the decolonization of knowledge: Prepared for the Canadian Commission for UNESCO.* https://en.ccunesco.ca/-/media/Files/Unesco/Resources/2020/07/OpenScienceDecolonizingKnowledge.pdf

Clavero, M. (2010). "Awkward wording. Rephrase": Linguistic injustice in ecological journals. *Trends in Ecology & Evolution, 25*(10), 552–553. 10.1016/j.tree.2010.07.001

Coady, D. (2010). Two concepts of epistemic injustice. *Episteme, 7*(2), 101–113. 10.3366/epi.2010.0001

Coady, D. (2017). Epistemic injustice as distributive injustice. In I. J. Kidd, J. Medina, & G. Pohlhaus (Eds.), *The Routledge handbook of epistemic injustice.* Routledge.

Cockerill, M. J., & Knols, B. G. J. (2008). Open access to research for the developing world. *Issues in Science and Technology, 24*(2), 65–69. https://www.jstor.org/stable/43314631

Cox, E. (2023). Research outputs as testimony and the APC as testimonial injustice in the Global South. *College & Research Libraries, 84*(4), 513–530. 10.5860/crl.84.4.513

Dotson, K. (2012). A cautionary tale: On limiting epistemic oppression. *Frontiers: A Journal of Women Studies, 33*(1), 24–47. 10.5250/fronjwomestud.33.1.0024

Dotson, K. (2014). Conceptualizing epistemic oppression. *Social Epistemology, 28*(2), 115–138. 10.1080/02691728.2013.782585

Elliott, K. C., & Resnik, D. B. (2019). Making open science work for science and society. *Environmental Health Perspectives, 127*(7), 075002. 10.1289/EHP4808

ElSabry, E. (2017). Who needs access to research? Exploring the societal impact of open access. *Revue Française Des Sciences de l'information et de La Communication, 11*. 10.4000/rfsic.3271

Eve, M., & Gray, J. (Eds.). (2020). *Reassembling scholarly communications: Histories, infrastructures, and global politics of open access.* MIT Press. 10.7551/mitpress/11885.001.0001

Fecher, B., Friesike, S., Hebing, M., & Linek, S. (2017). A reputation economy: How individual reward considerations trump systemic arguments for open access to data. *Palgrave Communications, 3*(1), 17051. 10.1057/palcomms.2017.51

Foucault, M. (1971). *The order of things: An archaeology of the human sciences (1st American ed.).* Pantheon Books.

Foucault, M. (1972). *The archaeology of knowledge.* Tavistock Publications.

Fowler, C. T. (2014). An editor's opinion on the ethics of open access. *Ethnobiology Letters, 5*, 1–3. https://www.jstor.org/stable/26423573

Fricker, M. (2007). *Epistemic injustice: Power and the ethics of knowing.* Oxford University Press.

Fricker, M. (2013). Epistemic justice as a condition of political freedom? *Synthese, 190*(7), 1317–1332. 10.1007/s11229-012-0227-3

Fricker, M. (2017). Evolving concepts of epistemic injustice. In I. J. Kidd, J. Medina, & G. Pohlhaus Jr (Eds.), *Routledge handbook of epistemic injustice* (pp. 53–60). Routledge. https://www.routledge.com/9781138882254

Gramsci, A. (1937). *Prison notebooks (J. A. Buttigieg, Ed.; A. Callari, Trans.).* Columbia University Press.

Gwynn, S. (2019). *Access to research in the global south: Reviewing the evidence.* INASP: International Network for the Availability of

Scientific Publications. https://www.inasp.info/publications/access-research-global-south-reviewing-evidence

Haider, J. (2007). Of the rich and the poor and other curious minds: On open access and "development". *Aslib Proceedings, 59*(4/5), 449–461. 10.1108/00012530710817636

Hampson, G. (2020). Common ground in the global quest for open research: Summary version. *Emerald Open Research, 2.* https://emeraldopenresearch.com/documents/2-18

Harle, J., & Warne, V. (2019). *Open access: Challenges and opportunities for low- and middle-income countries and the potential impact of UK policy.* International Network for International Network for Advancing Science and Policy (INASP) for the Foreign, Commonwealth & Development Office, UK. https://www.gov.uk/research-for-development-outputs/open-access-challenges-and-opportunities-for-low-and-middle-income-countries-and-the-potential-impact-of-uk-policy

Havemann, J., Bezuidenhout, L., Achampong, J., Akligoh, H., Ayodele, O., Hussein, S., Ksibi, N., Mboa Nkoudou, T. H., Obanda, J., Owango, J., Sanga, V. L., Stirling, J., & Wenzelmann, V. (2020). *Harnessing the open science infrastructure for an efficient African response to COVID-19.* Zenodo. 10.5281/ZENODO.3733768

Hookway, C. (2010). Some varieties of epistemic injustice: Reflections on Fricker. *Episteme, 7*(2), 151–163. 10.3366/epi.2010.0005

Kadakia, K. T., Beckman, A. L., Ross, J. S., & Krumholz, H. M. (2021). Leveraging open science to accelerate research. *New England Journal of Medicine, 384*(17), e61. 10.1056/NEJMp2034518

Knöchelmann, M. (2021). The democratisation myth: Open access and the solidification of epistemic injustices. *Science & Technology Studies, 34*(2), Article 2. 10.23987/sts.94964

Kwon, D. (2022). Open-access publishing fees deter researchers in the global south. *Nature, 603*(7903). 10.1038/d41586-022-00342-w

Mboa Nkoudou, T. H. (2020). Epistemic alienation in African scholarly communications: Open access as a pharmakon. In M. P. Eve & J. Gray (Eds.), *Reassembling scholarly communications: Histories, infrastructures, and global politics of open access.* MIT Press. 10.7551/mitpress/11885.003.0006

Meagher, K. (2021). Introduction: The politics of open access—Decolonizing research or corporate capture? *Development and Change, 52*(2), 340–358. 10.1111/dech.12630

Mering, M. (2020). Open access mandates and policies: The basics. *Serials Review, 46*(2), 157–159. 10.1080/00987913.2020.1760707

Minniti, S., Santoro, V., & Belli, S. (2018). Mapping the development of open access in Latin America and Caribbean countries. An analysis of Web of Science Core Collection and SciELO Citation Index (2005–2017). *Scientometrics, 117*(3), 1905–1930. 10.1007/s11192-018-2950-0

Mwangi, K. W., Mainye, N., Ouso, D. O., Esoh, K., Muraya, A. W., Mwangi, C. K., Naitore, C., Karega, P., Kibet-Rono, G., Musundi, S., Mutisya, J., Mwangi, E., Mgawe, C., Miruka, S., Kibet, C. K., & OpenScienceKE Collaborators. (2021). Open science in Kenya: Where are we? *Frontiers in Research Metrics and Analytics, 6.* https://www.frontiersin.org/articles/10.3389/frma.2021.669675

Okafor, I. A., Mbagwu, S. I., Chia, T., Hasim, Z., Udokanma, E. E., & Chandran, K. (2022). Institutionalizing open science in Africa: Limitations and prospects. *Frontiers in Research Metrics and Analytics, 7.* https://www.frontiersin.org/articles/10.3389/frma.2022.855198

Pinfield, S., Wakeling, S., Bawden, D., & Robinson, L. (2020). *Open access in theory and practice: The theory-practice relationship and openness*. Routledge. 10.4324/9780429276842

Piron, F. (2018). Postcolonial open access. In U. Herb & J. Schopfel (Eds.), *Open divide: Critical studies in open access*. Litwin Books. http://hdl.handle.net/20.500.11794/16178

Piron, F., Olyhoek, T., Vilchis, I. L., Smith, I., & Liré, Z. (2021). Saying 'no' to rankings and metrics: Scholarly communication and knowledge democracy. In B. L. Hall & R. Tandon (Eds.), *Socially responsible higher education* (pp. 80–91). Brill. 10.1163/9789004459076_007

Raju, R., Claassen, J., Pietersen, J., & Abrahamse, D. (2020). An authentic flip subscription model for Africa: Library as publisher service. *Library Management, 41*(6/7), 369–381. 10.1108/LM-03-2020-0054

Rodrigues, M. L., Savino, W., & Goldenberg, S. (2022). Article-processing charges as a barrier for science in low-to-medium income regions. *Memórias Do Instituto Oswaldo Cruz, 117*, e220064. 10.1590/0074-02760220064

Scherlen, A., & Robinson, M. (2008). Open access to criminal justice scholarship: A matter of social justice. *Journal of Criminal Justice Education, 19*(1), 54–74. 10.1080/10511250801892961

Science Europe. (2022). *Open science as part of a well-functioning research system*. Science Europe. https://www.scienceeurope.org/our-resources/direction-paper-open-science/

Sengupta, P. (2021). Open access publication: Academic colonialism or knowledge philanthropy? *Geoforum, 118*(1), 203–206. 10.1016/j.geoforum.2020.04.001

Yamey, G. (2008). Excluding the poor from accessing biomedical literature: A rights violation that impedes global health. *Health and Human Rights, 10*(1), 21–42. 10.2307/20460085

3   Scientific openness as a starting point

In this chapter, I want to explore some of the fundamental presumptions that underlie the case, as it has often been made, for open access. This will help us to begin to explore arguments for OA, which I contend are commonly based on an essentially positivist view of science, which sees scientific knowledge as normative and universal. The question of the relationship between the case for OA and ideas about knowledge itself – what constitutes valid and valuable knowledge – will underlie a great deal of the discussion in this book. I will relate the common arguments for OA (and open science more broadly) to Robert Merton's influential scientific norms. The social and political context within which Merton was working, of mid-20th-century liberalism, then comes into view, and it is notable that liberal theory is the philosophical basis that implicitly underpins the case for OA as it is often made. I will suggest these widely used arguments for OA, although helpful in many ways, only get us so far. They are, however, an important starting point, and help to establish some key principles of the case for OA that are often taken for granted, including the universal value of scientific outputs and OA as a form of distributive epistemic justice, which I will discuss.

Normative views of scientific knowledge

It is important to note early a key presumption underpinning the OA movement: the presumption of the universal validity and value of scientific knowledge. Open access to scientific content is important because the knowledge that it makes globally available is universally valid and valuable, at least in some sense. Otherwise, there would be little point in sharing it openly. This is such an obvious aspect of the rationale for OA that it almost goes without saying. However, as I hope will become clear, it *is* important to say it, since many of the critiques of OA are based on meta-theoretical foundations that problematise the validity and value of scientific knowledge. Of course, in order to argue that scientific outputs have universal validity and value, it is not necessary to

DOI: 10.4324/9781032679259-3

argue that *every* scientific output is itself valid and valuable, but rather that the knowledge system within which such outputs are generated is.

Since the assumption about the importance of scientific knowledge underpins much of the case for OA (that scientific knowledge is worth sharing), controversies about open access are bound up with debates about different forms of knowledge themselves, and the extent to which we see them as valid and valuable. I am using the word 'knowledge' to mean justified belief. In the case of scientific knowledge, there are often formalised ways of providing justification to demonstrate the veridicality of knowledge claims (e.g., peer review processes), and formalised modes of codifying and communicating that knowledge (e.g., journal articles). I will go on to discuss different types of knowledge, different kinds of approaches to the justification of knowledge claims, and different modes of codifying and communicating knowledge, as this book progresses. By 'valid' knowledge, I mean that which is recognised as demonstrably reliable and trustworthy. There may be different standards and processes by which we can demonstrate the reliability and trustworthiness of knowledge, which enable the recognition of its validity. By 'valuable' knowledge, I mean that which we understand to be significant and useful. There are different kinds of value: scientific, social, economic, and other kinds – economic value is only one of the different kinds of value to which I am referring.

We have already seen that many critiques of OA are not just critiques of business models and academic practices, but also critiques of the knowledge being made OA – of the types of knowledge made available in conventional scholarly publications, of the perceived validity of such knowledge, and the value placed on it, and of who gets to say what is valid and valuable. Different views of knowledge are commonly implicit in debates on OA and OS, but they often become more obvious in discussions of critiques of global OA as a form of epistemic injustice and oppression (introduced in Chapter 2). The argument that scientific knowledge is universally valid, and that sharing it via open access channels is a universal good, stands against the argument that science is Western knowledge used as an oppressive force against non-Western peoples, an injustice which is exacerbated by OA. Putting it like that makes it clear that this is not just an argument about OA but an argument about knowledge itself. It is therefore important for us here to unpack and disentangle the arguments in some detail. Doing so requires us to drill down into meta-theory, involving fundamental questions of ontology (concerning reality and existence) and epistemology (concerning knowledge and what we can know), and see how they relate to openness.

Underlying the arguments of many OA advocates is often an implicit normative view of scientific knowledge – scientific knowledge is universal (that is, not subject to local contexts) and non-temporal (that is, not subject to historical contingencies). This is based on well-established theories of science articulated by influential modernist thinkers, such as Merton (1973) and Popper (1959), although going back much further. The arguments of many OA advocates can be inferred to be based on an essentially positivist paradigm. In simple terms, positivism consists of a realist ontology and objectivist epistemology: that there is a real world 'out there', separate from our own perceptions of it, and that it can be known, measured, and understood (Park et al., 2020). Reality is known through verifiable facts established by observation and measurement, then understood through the development of explanatory theory. Theory can in turn be confirmed, developed, or overturned through hypotheses tested by further observation and measurement. This is a particular kind of realism, which might be called empiricist realism, one that is based on confidence in the observability and comprehensibility of reality. At the core of this meta-theoretical approach is the notion of causal regularity, where causal relationships can be observed, often through controlled experiments which are used to test and record the relationships between entities. Experiments are normally approached through the hypothetico-deductive method, in which hypotheses are tested against experimental data, which either confirm or falsify the hypotheses. Produced in this way, scientific knowledge is seen as objective, empirically verifiable, and universally valid.

The positivist paradigm has been qualified in various ways, resulting in different versions of rationalist adapted- or neo-positivism, which may recognise the subjectivity of the researcher (Popper, 1959), the provisionality of scientific knowledge (Polanyi, 1958) or its historical contingency (Kuhn, 1996). Such qualifications are, however, often made partly to help researchers recognise and minimise the effect of these issues in their practice – researchers need to be aware of their subjectivity, for example, to develop strategies that help to reduce the possibility of biases influencing their work. Kinds of positivism remain the basic paradigm within which most STEMM (science, technology, engineering, mathematics, and medicine) research is undertaken, and is rarely questioned by STEMM researchers themselves (Miedema, 2022). (Adapted-) positivism also underpins certain types of social sciences research, particularly quantitative empirical social studies (Crook & Garratt, 2005).

Positivism in its different forms often involves a kind of epistemic confidence, which valorises certain types of knowledge as superior – specifically empirical, quantitative knowledge produced through scientific investigation – and other forms of knowledge inferior. A clear view of the resulting hierarchy of knowledge types can be seen in biomedical evidence-based 'pyramids' (Djulbegovic & Guyatt, 2017). Systematic reviews of quantitative studies are ranked highest, followed by randomised controlled trials, and then other types of quantitative studies. Qualitative studies often do not even feature in such hierarchies and if they do, they are situated at the bottom of the pyramid. Such (adapted-) positivism sometimes comes with a triumphalist tone. It is often associated with modernism and 20th-century Western industrialised power, characterised by confidence in science and technology, and the ability of human societies to shape and exploit their own environment.

Many of OA's early advocates seem often to have been working within an (adapted-) positivist paradigm. They regularly presented the benefits of OA in terms of making the literature widely available across different global regions through disciplinary perspectives such as medical and health sciences, computer sciences and physics (Barbour et al., 2006; Walport & Kiley, 2006). Such arguments for OA have often had a positivist flavour, particularly the assumption of the universality of scientific knowledge, and global benefits in sharing it. In a joint editorial between the *Bulletin of the World Health Organization* and the OA journal, *PLoS Medicine*, Barbour et al. (2006) wrote that one of the key benefits of changing scholarly communication to work on a more open basis would be improvements in health care and policy:

The potential benefits of such a change are vast. No longer will physicians have to base their practice on half truths. Instead, everyone from patients to policymakers can read for themselves the evidence on which crucial science and health policy decisions are made. One example of a paper with potentially profound public health implications is the first randomized trial of male circumcision to prevent HIV infection; having this paper and all related discussions freely available has allowed a lively, informed debate to flourish.

(Barbour et al., 2006, p. 339)

As far as many OA advocates working within this frame are concerned, OA has an essentially inclusive agenda – with clear aims to make research outputs more widely accessible (for readers) but also to allow a broad variety of researchers to contribute to the scientific corpus (as authors) – the "lively and informed debate", referred to by Barbour et al. (2006), which might also involve clinicians, policymakers and others. However, it is important to note that this inclusive agenda focuses on widening access and enabling contributions to the conventional scientific corpus (Fonn et al., 2018). The knowledge system to which access is being provided, or to which contribution is being encouraged, remains the same, regardless of the global location of the researcher or the culture within which they live.

This is usually the implicit context for common instrumental arguments for OA. The scientific system works through communication – it is essential that new findings are disseminated as widely as possible so they can be read, tested, and built on by other scientists. OA is a mechanism for making the system more effective by, for example, widening access to knowledge and accelerating its dissemination. It can be made more efficient by reducing costs and ensuring value is achieved for public spending (Johnson, 2005). This argument has been explored and elaborated in all sorts of ways, for instance, in investigating costs associated with publishing, establishing new business models, or experimenting with new technologies that enable openness (Grossmann & Brembs, 2021; Padula et al., 2017; Schimmer et al., 2015). All of this is significant, and I would argue, fundamentally credible and helpful, but it is important to note for our current purposes that it assumes a well-understood model of science, based on established (arguably, Western) norms, and on meta-theory which assumes the universality of scientific knowledge and the global value of scientific outputs. It is this knowledge, the argument goes, that needs to be made more open.

Merton's scientific norms

The norms of science produced by the sociologist and philosopher of science, Robert Merton, have been influential in adapted-positivist modernist thinking in relation to scientific practices. They have been used to reinforce arguments for open access and open science (Fecher et al., 2017; Vicente-Saez et al., 2021). In his paper, 'The Normative Structure of Science' (1942, 1973), Merton identified four norms that underpin the way science should be done: "universalism", "communism", "disinterestedness", and "organised scepticism". Each of these can be seen as having implications for scholarly communication and open access.

The principle of universalism is based on the idea that scientific knowledge can and should be impersonal and objective. Science requires researchers to remove their own subjective perspectives and be as objective as possible in order to establish universal knowledge. Scientists should resist particularism and ethnocentrism. Scientists can be based anywhere in the world, and the principle of universalism, Merton observes, should mean that science is "open to talents" regardless of their origin. Scientists should be recruited based on talent and merit, rather than social status or other external factors. Merton sees this as fundamentally "democratic" and resistant to pressures of social conventions or from authoritarian regimes.

This leads to the principle of communism. The communism Merton refers to relates to science as a shared endeavour: "the substantive findings of science are a product of social collaboration and are assigned to the community" (Merton, 1973, p. 273). He recognises scientists act competitively to accrue status and reputation, but they do so by sharing their findings. Communication of findings is therefore crucial, with Merton advocating "full and open communication". By "open communication" Merton was not, of course, referring to what we today call open access, but it is clear his ideas have implications for contemporary OA approaches. OA seems to be a way of effectively enacting this principle.

The norm of disinterestedness emphasises the need to focus impartially on science in its own right, rather than pursuing other personal, political or ideological agendas through science. A key issue associated with disinterestedness is that of integrity in science: conducting science and science communication in a way that can be trusted by others. Merton argues that integrity needs to be combined with competition in reputation-building, in which all scientists engage, so that scientists have to earn the trust of their community, by providing evidence of their integrity and the soundness of their methods, in order to compete successfully.

The final Mertonian norm, organised scepticism, refers to how scientific processes are set up to test and challenge claims. Merton applies this to science and scientific institutions, involving "the temporary suspension of judgement and the detached scrutiny of beliefs" (Merton, 1973, p. 277), something which we can see is built into practices such as peer review of funding proposals and scientific outputs. He also applies the principle to the relationship between science and wider society, once again referring to the way the scientific community should resist external political or ideological pressures.

There are obvious connections between Merton's norms and open access. These are perhaps most obvious in the principle of scientific communism. The principle that favours open communication could arguably be most effectively operationalised in an open access environment. Also, openness itself makes sense in the light of the principle of universalism – sharing is useful if what is being shared is universally valuable. Merton's principles resonate with other aspects of open science. For example, the need for scientific integrity (encompassed by the disinterestedness principle) has been an impetus for parts of the open science movement. Greater openness in scientific practices, such as data sharing, is often seen as a vehicle for enabling reproducibility, a key component of assuring scientific integrity. The principles of disinterestedness and organised scepticism also connect with important issues prominent in the open science movement, manifested in open peer review, amongst other things.

It is important to understand that these principles arose out of a particular context. Merton was writing during and after the Second World War, living in a liberal democracy, a kind of social order at that time under threat. He frames many of his ideas in a way that reflects this context, particularly in his account of the relationship between science and wider society. His references to scientists being pressured by external actors implicitly refer to relations between the scientific community and Hitler's Nazi regime. Nevertheless, his ideas have been influential throughout the global science community ever since, and have often been used as a kind of baseline in discussing the culture and conduct of science (Vicente-Saez et al., 2021).

Open society liberalism

Merton developed his approach to science, including his four principles, in the frame of liberal social theory – his essay on the normative structure of science was originally published under the title, 'Science and Technology in a Democratic Order' (Merton, 1942, 1973). This framing has influenced how the case for OA itself has often been discussed – and leads us now to bring social theory into our considerations. In introducing social theory, it is important to note its relationship with meta-theory. As well as describing world views undergirding scientific research, meta-theory acts as a foundation for theories designed to explain social, cultural, economic, and other phenomena investigated by social scientists and others. Social theory is not suspended in epistemological mid-air, but is always built on meta-theoretical foundations, whether acknowledged or not. Any consideration of how social theory can be used to understand phenomena, therefore, should involve maintaining an awareness of the meta-theoretical foundations on which any social theory is constructed.

The argument for effectiveness and efficiency made in relation to OA has resonance in liberal social theory, as do arguments around transparency and accountability (Davis, 2009; Miedema, 2022). Transparency and accountability are often seen as important for maintaining democratic institutions and processes, and an informed citizenry who can participate in them. In work closely related to Merton's, Karl Popper (1945) developed the ideal of the "open society", characterised by individualistic liberal democracy, in contrast to the "closed" totalitarian regimes and societies of the mid-20th century. It was Popper's work, along with economists like Friedrich Hayek (1944), that portrayed the free market and liberal democracy as important complementary elements of an open society. An open society is also characterised by freedom of speech and freedom of the press and other media. Freedom of information in various forms is additionally often seen as important in an open society. Such liberalism is closely associated with a model of openness that Peters and Roberts (2012) call the "open market society". Leonelli (2023) comments:

Openness has long been a guiding principle for liberal democracies, where recognition of the epistemic significance of transparent, free and inclusive inquiry is a source of both political and scientific legitimacy.
(Leonelli, 2023, p. 1)

The billionaire philanthropist, George Soros, has promoted this strand of thinking about openness, in founding the Open Society Institute, which sponsored the BOAI. Soros has acknowledged his debt to Popper, although he has questioned Popper's optimism that greater openness of political discourse would necessarily promote democracy without other safeguards (Soros, 2011). From this perspective, open access in science is one strand of a wider open society, which, amongst other things, enables transparency and fuels economic growth in a knowledge economy. This frame of openness often gives particular emphasis to the value of scientific knowledge in economic terms, with accompanying emphasis on apparatus such as legal protections of intellectual property and copyright measures designed to enable the exploitation of the content as a financial asset (Peukert & Sonnenberg, 2017). It is arguably this understanding of knowledge that has given rise to the "knowledge market" version of OA, dominated as it now is by large commercial corporations and sustained by for-profit business models, such as APCs (Pinfield et al., 2020). Some advocates of OA implicitly working within this liberal frame express worries about the oligopolistic nature of the publishing market, anatomised by Larivière et al. (2015), but, crucially, have traditionally seen creating a more competitive market as the solution to the problem (Brembs et al., 2023; Velterop, 2001).

It is all too easy to be cynical about this "open society" model of OA and open science, and of the claims that its advocates are motivated by what Hampson (2020a) calls "idealism". I would suggest, however, that as we see more countries retreating into a kind of scientific nationalism, turning their science system in on themselves for nationalistic reasons – witness China's scientific inward policy turn in the wake of the COVID-19 pandemic (Mallapaty, 2023) – it is important to recognise the value of the "open society" model. This is particularly the case since the liberal model involves a commitment to address distributive epistemic injustice, "the unfair distribution of epistemic goods such as education or information" (Fricker, 2013, p. 1318). OA is often born of a liberal impulse. Fricker (2013) makes the key point that distributive epistemic justice is closely linked to liberal ideals of political freedom and justice. The link with distributive epistemic justice may not be obvious in the literature, since many OA advocates, making an essentially liberal argument, do not often use the language of 'justice', often preferring 'public good' or 'societal impact' (Hampson, 2020b). Nevertheless, OA provides greater access to a range of epistemic resources regardless of ability to pay. It is important to note, therefore, that the argument from epistemic justice in relation to OA is not the monopoly of OA's critics. Critics have tended to focus on discriminatory epistemic injustice, which we will explore later. Nevertheless, we should recognise at this stage that the argument for scientific openness is an argument for addressing epistemic injustice – distributive epistemic injustice – and has always been that, even if not always described in those terms.

However, some critiques of OA, as we have seen, portray the current state of open scholarly communication differently – not as a vehicle for distributive justice, but as one way in which the Global North achieves dominance over the Global South. The criticism often also applies to the version of liberalism on which the case for OA is commonly based. Piron (2018) draws a comparison between OA and development aid, treating both with equal suspicion. This is an interesting analogy, which in many ways helps us to understand the argument about the relationship between OA and liberalism. Working within a liberal frame, many would favour sending development aid to LMICs, and, despite its problems, would see development aid as likely to lead to positive outcomes, at least in many circumstances (Dercon, 2022). Drake et al. (2023) argue that open access itself is a development issue, since access to scientific knowledge can play a role in driving development in LMICs. However, Piron sees parallels between aid and OA in a negative light, regarding both as vehicles of Northern hegemonic power exercised over the Global South (Piron, 2018). Drawing on established aid-sceptical thought, which argues aid is at best ineffective and at worst a mask for exploitation (Engel, 2014; Gulrajani, 2011), Piron contends that the case for aid is often based on a misleading narrative of "catching up". The Global South needs simply to "catch up" with Global North economic development based on the implicit goal of capitalist modernity, with development aid given on that understanding. The 'catch up' view also operates in science: the assumption being that the Global South simply needs to catch up with science in the Global North. This thinking, Piron argues, often underpins the liberal case for OA: OA will help the Global South to catch up. Piron criticises such a view as being based on a universalist "positivist perspective" of science, a position she wants to replace with a more "critical" perspective, based on an understanding of knowledge as contextual and situated.

If one adopts the critical perspective, then African science should be African knowledge anchored in African contexts and using African epistemologies to answer African questions, while also using other knowledge from the rest of the world, including Western science if relevant.

(Piron, 2018, p. 120)

It is this notion of a different kind of science, one which challenges positivist universalism, that we will go on to consider in the following chapters of this book, including an exploration of how it relates to the case for openness. Many of those who take a postcolonial critical perspective on OA also favour inclusion in scholarly communication of radically different epistemic systems from those underpinning much of Western science, something we will also explore as this book progresses.

However, it is important to emphasise at this point that many of the critics of OA, including Piron, are not opposed to OA as such. I will go on to discuss some of the meta-theoretical underpinnings of the theory on which much of the critique of OA is based, which questions the (adapted-) positivist position on knowledge. However, for now, I want to observe that many critics of OA who use critical or postcolonial theory advocate the reformation of the OA agenda, rather than its abolition. They advocate what they see as a different kind of openness, often involving ensuring OA is implemented in certain ways, using sustainable business and funding models, and allowing for different kinds of science. In doing so, they typically point to models of OA in the Global South as being exemplary. In South America, for example, the SciELO service was set up before the BOAI and is still an important part of the global OA infrastructure (Packer, 2020). The RedALyC platform was set up 2003, also in Latin America (Becerril-García & Aguado-López, 2019). Both deploy a "knowledge commons" rather than a "knowledge market" model (Capps, 2021; Pinfield et al., 2020). In line with this, I also will be arguing for more equitable business and sustainability models of OA being urgently required for global openness to thrive. I will come back to this issue in Chapter 8 when we look at participatory openness.

One additional point is worth making explicit at this stage in relation to any drive to create a more equitable global OA around "knowledge commons" models referencing developments like SciELO and RedALyC. The point is this: OA itself is not an invention of the Global North imposed on the Global South. There is growing recognition that many aspects of OA developed earlier and are more embedded in low- and middle-income countries than in high-income countries (Minniti et al., 2018). At an institutional level, evidence suggests many universities in South America and Asia have reached higher levels of OA adoption than those in Europe and North America (Huang et al., 2020). The same applies to disciplinary communities, such as the life sciences (Iyandemye & Thomas, 2019), where researchers in LMICs make a greater proportion of their outputs openly available than their counterparts in HICs. Recognising the fact that OA is widely supported and adopted in LMICs is important in our understanding of scientific openness, and it can also help us begin to understand my next key point: the case for epistemic openness. This is discussed in the following chapter.

References

Barbour, V., Chinnock, P., Cohen, B., & Yamey, G. (2006). The impact of open access upon public health. *Bulletin of the World Health Organization, 84*(5), 339–339. 10.2471/BLT.06.032409

Becerril-García, A., & Aguado-López, E. (2019). The end of a centralized open access project and the beginning of a community-based sustainable infrastructure for Latin America: Redalyc.org after Fifteen Years. In L. Chan & P. Mounier (Eds.), *Connecting the Knowledge Commons—From Projects to Sustainable Infrastructure: The 22nd International Conference on Electronic Publishing – Revised Selected Papers* (pp. 41–55). OpenEdition Press. 10.4000/books.oep.9003

Brembs, B., Huneman, P., Schönbrodt, F., Nilsonne, G., Susi, T., Siems, R., Perakakis, P., Trachana, V., Ma, L., & Rodriguez-Cuadrado, S. (2023). Replacing academic journals. *Royal Society Open Science. 10*(7). 10.5281/zenodo.7643806

Capps, B. (2021). Where does open science lead us during a pandemic? A public good argument to prioritize rights in the open commons. *Cambridge Quarterly of Healthcare Ethics, 30*(1), 11–24. 10.1017/S0963180120000456

Crook, C., & Garratt, D. (2005). The positivist paradigm in contemporary social science research. In B. Somekh & C. Lewin (Eds.), *Research methods in the social sciences* (pp. 207–214). Sage.

Davis, P. M. (2009). How the media frames 'open access'. *Journal of Electronic Publishing, 12*(1). 10.3998/3336451.0012.101

Dercon, S. (2022). *Gambling on development: Why some countries win and others lose.* Hurst & Company.

Djulbegovic, B., & Guyatt, G. H. (2017). Progress in evidence-based medicine: A quarter century on. *The Lancet, 390*(10092), 415–423. 10.1016/S0140-6736(16)315 92-6

Drake, T., Gulliver, S., & Harle, J. (2023). *Research publishing is an under-recognised global challenge: Opportunities for the G20 to act (306; CGD Policy Paper).* Center for Global Development. https://www.cgdev.org/publication/research-publishing-under-recognised-global-challenge-opportunities-g20-act

Engel, S. (2014). The not-so-great aid debate. *Third World Quarterly, 35*(8), 1374–1389. 10.1080/01436597.2014.946251

Fecher, B., Friesike, S., Hebing, M., & Linek, S. (2017). A reputation economy: How individual reward considerations trump systemic arguments for open access to data. *Palgrave Communications, 3*(1), 17051. 10.1057/palcomms.2017.51

Fonn, S., Ayiro, L. P., Cotton, P., Habib, A., Mbithi, P. M. F., Mtenje, A., Nawangwe, B., Ogunbodede, E. O., Olayinka, I., Golooba-Mutebi, F., & Ezeh, A. (2018). Repositioning Africa in global knowledge production. *The Lancet, 392*(10153), 1163–1166. 10.1016/S0140-6736(18)31068-7

Fricker, M. (2013). Epistemic justice as a condition of political freedom? *Synthese, 190*(7), 1317–1332. 10.1007/s11229-012-0227-3

Grossmann, A., & Brembs, B. (2021). Current market rates for scholarly publishing services. *F1000Research, 10.* 10.12688/f1000research.27468.2

Gulrajani, N. (2011). Transcending the great foreign aid debate: Managerialism, radicalism and the search for aid effectiveness. *Third World Quarterly, 32*(2), 199–216. 10.1080/01436597.2011.560465

Hampson, G. (2020a). *Common ground in the global quest for open research (OSI Policy Perspective 2).* Open Scholarship Initiative: Science Communication Institute and Mason Publishing. 10.13021/osi2020.2725

Hampson, G. (2020b). Common ground in the global quest for open research: Summary version. *Emerald Open Research, 2.* https://emeraldopenresearch.com/documents/2-18

Hayek, F. A. (1944). *The road to serfdom*. Routledge.

Huang, C. K., Neylon, C., Hosking, R., Montgomery, L., Wilson, K. S., Ozaygen, A., & Brookes-Kenworthy, C. (2020). Evaluating the impact of open access policies on research institutions. *eLife, 9*, 1–13. 10.7554/ELIFE.57067

Iyandemye, J., & Thomas, M. P. (2019). Low income countries have the highest percentages of open access publication: A systematic computational analysis of the biomedical literature. *PLoS One, 14*(7), e0220229. 10.1371/journal.pone.0220229

Johnson, R. K. (2005). Open access: Unlocking the value of scientific research. *Journal of Library Administration, 42*(2), 107–124. 10.1300/J111v42n02_08

Kuhn, T. S. (1996). *The structure of scientific revolutions (3rd ed)*. University of Chicago Press.

Larivière, V., Haustein, S., & Mongeon, P. (2015). The oligopoly of academic publishers in the digital era. *PLoS One, 10*(6), e0127502. 10.1371/journal.pone.0127502

Leonelli, S. (2023). *Philosophy of open science*. Cambridge University Press. 10.1017/9781009416368

Mallapaty, S. (2023). China is mobilizing science to spur development—And self-reliance. *Nature, 615*(7953), 570–571. 10.1038/d41586-023-00744-4

Merton, R. K. (1942). Science and technology in a democratic order. *Journal of Legal and Political Sociology, 1*(1), 115–126.

Merton, R. K. (1973). *The sociology of science: Theoretical and empirical investigations* (N. W. Storer, Ed.). University of Chicago Press. https://archive.org/details/sociologyofscien0000mert

Miedema, F. (2022). *Open science: The very idea*. Springer Netherlands. 10.1007/978-94-024-2115-6

Minniti, S., Santoro, V., & Belli, S. (2018). Mapping the development of open access in Latin America and Caribbean countries. An analysis of Web of Science Core Collection and SciELO Citation Index (2005–2017). *Scientometrics, 117*(3), 1905–1930. 10.1007/s11192-018-2950-0

Packer, A. (2020). The pasts, presents, and futures of SciELO. In M. P. Eve & J. Gray (Eds.), *Reassembling scholarly communications: Histories, infrastructures, and global politics of open access* (pp. 297–313). MIT Press. 10.7551/mitpress/11885.003.0030

Padula, D., Brembs, B., Harnad, S., Herb, U., Missingham, R., Morgan, D., & Ortbal, J. (2017). *Democratizing academic journals: Technology, services, and open access*. Scholastica. https://s3.amazonaws.com/marketing.scholasticahq.com/Democratizing-Journal-Pub-WP.pdf

Park, Y. S., Konge, L., & Artino, A. R. J. (2020). The positivism paradigm of research. *Academic Medicine, 95*(5), 690. 10.1097/ACM.0000000000003093

Peters, M., & Roberts, P. (2012). *The virtues of openness: Education, science, and scholarship in the digital age*. Paradigm Publishers.

Peukert, A., & Sonnenberg, M. (2017). Copyright and changing systems of scientific communication. In P. Weingart & N. Taubert (Eds.), *The future of scholarly publishing: Open access and the economics of digitisation* (pp. 199–227). African Minds.

Pinfield, S., Wakeling, S., Bawden, D., & Robinson, L. (2020). *Open access in theory and practice: The theory-practice relationship and openness*. Routledge. 10.4324/9780429276842

Piron, F. (2018). Postcolonial open access. In U. Herb & J. Schopfel (Eds.), *Open divide: Critical studies in open access*. Litwin Books. http://hdl.handle.net/20.500.11794/16178

Polanyi, M. (1958). *Personal knowledge: Towards a post-critical philosophy*. Routledge and Kegan Paul.

Popper, K. (1945). *The open society and its enemies.* Routledge and Kegan Paul.

Popper, K. (1959). *The logic of scientific discovery.* Hutchinson.

Schimmer, R., Geschuhn, K. K., & Vogler, A. (2015). *Disrupting the subscription journals' business model for the necessary large-scale transformation to open access: A Max Planck Digital Library open access policy white paper.* Max Planck Society. 10.17617/1.3

Soros, G. (2011, June 23). My philanthropy. *New York Review of Books.* https://www.nybooks.com/articles/2011/06/23/my-philanthropy/

Velterop, J. (2001). Who is prepared to pay, and how much? *Nature, 411*(6838), 633–633. 10.1038/35079766

Vicente-Saez, R., Gustafsson, R., & Martinez-Fuentes, C. (2021). Opening up science for a sustainable world: An expansive normative structure of open science in the digital era. *Science and Public Policy, 48*(6), 799–813. 10.1093/scipol/scab049

Walport, M., & Kiley, R. (2006). Open access, UK PubMed Central and the Wellcome Trust. *Journal of the Royal Society of Medicine, 99*(9), 438–439. 10.1258/jrsm.99.9.438

4 Epistemic openness and constructionism

In this chapter, I will start by discussing some of the problems to which (adapted-) positivism gives rise and how constructionist meta-theory has been developed in response. This will help us begin to recognise the ostensible case for greater epistemic openness, which I am arguing should accompany scientific openness. To make this case, I also need to discuss what is included in the category of 'science' and then how science relates to other forms of knowledge. I am going to argue for the benefits of widening our epistemic boundaries, and that doing so can help us begin to address hermeneutical epistemic injustices in scholarly communication. I will provide some initial examples of what such epistemic openness can look like, including engagement between conventional scientific knowledge and indigenous knowledges from countries and cultures in LMICs. These examples will, I hope, begin to make the case for how epistemic openness can usefully complement open access and other forms of scientific openness.

Constructionism and widening epistemic boundaries

We need at this stage to return to the meta-theoretical foundations of OA and of the value we place on different forms of knowledge. The argument for epistemic openness, to complement open access and other forms of scientific openness, is based on awareness of the problems of (adapted-) positivist ideas of knowledge. One fundamental problem is the conflation of ontology and epistemology: treating reality and our knowledge of it as one and the same thing. In the (adapted-) positivist paradigm, scientific knowledge is assumed to be a direct description of reality, and this can lead to unwarranted confidence in scientific knowledge as indisputable fact. The empiricist realism on which this confidence is based is questionable, relying as it does on the ideas of observational objectivity and fact-theory separation, both of which are problematic.

As far as observational objectivity is concerned, as Rivas (2010) puts it: "by definition, observation data are not independent of observation,

DOI: 10.4324/9781032679259-4

and therefore cannot be objective" (p. 210). All knowledge, including scientific knowledge, is perspectival. Recognising this is a crucial aspect of many of the criticisms of positivism. Since observation is always carried out from a particular perspective, it is also likely to be coloured by the observer's prior knowledge. Any perspective involves presuppositions about what is being observed and why it is important. Separating observation and theory is in most cases impossible. Scientific facts are established within the context of theory, rather than being independent of theory, with the two always being entangled rather than readily separable.

Scientific theories are maps of reality, not reality itself. Even if well-developed, they are partial schematics or indicative patterns that attempt to fit together and interpret data in the most plausible way. Although sometimes not acknowledged, scientific theories are often formed or refined abductively as well as deductively (McKaughan, 2008; McMullin, 1992). An abductive approach involves drawing inferences from data to construct the best explanation – a creative, constructive process. Scientific theories are always subject to change. In response to new data, theories are revised or replaced over time, making the idea that scientific explanations are direct descriptions of an external reality difficult to maintain.

The ways in which theory is developed may often depend more on social and other contingent factors than is often assumed. One example is that of values. As Sayer (2012) observes:

> *For positivists, facts and values are different and incommensurable, and values are not logically deducible from facts. Given this, they argue that normative statements (oughts), about what is good or bad should therefore be avoided; 'no ought from is' is the slogan. Further they assume that values are a source of bias or contamination; as Weber (1946, p. 146) famously put it: 'Whenever the person of science introduces his personal value judgment, a full understanding of the facts ceases'. Positivists therefore argue that normative judgements threaten the objectivity of science and consequently must be excluded from its internal arguments and accounts as far as possible.*
>
> (Sayer, 2012, pp. 188–189)

Yet science and scientists are always influenced by values (consciously or otherwise), and whilst the role of values in science is the subject of considerable debate, it is difficult to argue that they are not important, even if you argue that ideally, they should not be (Elliott, 2022; Oreskes, 2019). Oreskes (2019) shows how it is difficult to maintain value-neutrality in science when thinking about issues such as the utility of science (e.g., potential health benefits which may motivate research) or questions of integrity in science (e.g., the need to maintain honesty and transparency in science). She also argues that values in science are important for creating and maintaining public trust in science, with scientists increasingly recognising that demonstrating shared values with people elsewhere in society is an important part of building a societal consensus that science is trustworthy.

In its 'hardest' forms, positivism can involve a failure to acknowledge sufficiently the limitations of scientific knowledge and a corresponding dismissive attitude to other forms of knowledge. Positivism easily slides into scientism – asserting that the only valid form of knowledge is that which is known, or can be known, through scientific investigation, such as that carried out in the physical and life sciences (Sorell, 1994). However, we know that many issues most important to us – ranging from the ethical (how should we behave?), through the political (how should we govern ourselves?) to the experiential (does my wife love me?) – cannot be answered by the scientific method, narrowly conceived. At the same time, social systems, like cultures or institutions, are also not easily understood through a positivist lens, based as they are on human perceptions and values. Positivist analysis of social systems often tends to be reductionist – breaking them down into individual and material constituent parts, without understanding the system (Sayer, 2010).

The problems with (adapted-) positivism seem to point to a need for a wider view of knowledge, involving a recognition that valid knowledge can take different forms. Other meta-theoretical frames, which have come to prominence as part of postmodern critiques of modernist positivism, involve such a recognition. As with (adapted-) positivism, anti-positivist perspectives are not easily summarised, because they can take a range of forms. However, what most of them have in common is the idea of the constructedness of knowledge. Our knowledge of reality is not something that is waiting to be discovered but is rather constructed through our individual perceptions and social experiences. All knowledge, including scientific knowledge, is created in particular contexts and contingent on particular circumstances (Kukla, 2000; Potter, 1996). Since it is situated in particular contexts rather than universal, knowledge is subjective and relative (Lincoln & Guba, 2016). The role of language and that of interactions between people and within communities are crucial in creating knowledge (Burr, 2015) and so it is on those things – linguistic issues and social interactions – that studies of knowledge generation often focus.

Constructionist accounts, therefore, tend to resist privileging certain forms of knowledge above others, and thus can constitute the basis of an argument for the need to respect different knowledge forms. Different kinds of knowledge have merit and can derive from different epistemic traditions. Such perspectives underpin a good deal of contemporary social sciences and humanities research, which often use ideas of the social construction of knowledge to explain the ways social systems and cultures work. These are areas where (adapted-) positivism most apparently struggles to provide credible explanations (Berger & Luckmann, 1966; Elder-Vass, 2012). Social systems can best be understood in ways that involve human perceptions and constructed knowledge. It is important in this case to recognise a range of forms of scientific and other knowledge forms, all of which can give us valuable insights.

Science and the boundaries of valid and valuable knowledge

We are not helped by the ambiguity of the word, 'science', an ambiguity often present in debates about OA. For many, 'science' refers, more or less, to the STEMM disciplines (science, technology, engineering, mathematics and medicine). Of course, built into the STEMM label itself is a finer distinction between 'science' and other disciplines, such as engineering or medicine. However, many people would argue that in broad terms all the STEMM disciplines, despite their differences, are based on shared ontological and epistemological assumptions, which often look like kinds of (adapted-) positivism. The borders between STEMM disciplines and others are, of course, fuzzy, but it is still common to distinguish STEMM from social sciences and humanities (SSH), just as it is also common to distinguish between and within social sciences and humanities themselves (Kagan, 2009).

On the other hand, some would refer to all these different types of formal scholarly knowledge (STEMM *and* SSH) as 'science', in the sense of 'Wissenschaft' (systematic academic knowledge). Extending the borders of scholarly knowledge this way militates against the kind of scientistic universalism already mentioned. It acknowledges that there are different forms of knowledge, and different kinds of epistemologies, characteristic of different disciplines, with different theories and methods (Becher & Trowler, 2001; Trowler et al., 2012). In addition, it is important to recognise that major differences are not necessarily captured entirely by disciplinary distinctions. Both within and across traditional disciplines, there are often significant commonalities and differences in practice (for example, methodological approaches), which can reflect varying views of what constitutes reliable knowledge (Gerson, 2013). Thinking this way can promote inter- and trans-disciplinary approaches, which can be valuable in addressing real-world research challenges, demonstrating the value of embracing different epistemic contributions (Vienni-Baptista et al., 2022).

Recognising the value of different epistemic systems evident within and between different disciplines that constitute 'science', in its broadest sense, is an important step in achieving the epistemic openness for which I am arguing. The recognition of the value of different kinds of knowledge systems is partly based on the meta-theoretical insight that knowledge is at least in some ways constructed (I will go on to discuss the limits of constructionism and its implications later). There are different kinds of knowing, even where knowledge is formalised in an academic context.

A powerful case for what she calls "epistemic diversity" in open science is made by Leonelli (2022). Her case is, I believe, compatible with my argument for epistemic openness. I see 'openness' as a means, and 'diversity' as an end. Leonelli helpfully identifies different sources of diversity, including "conceptual" (e.g., theoretical perspectives), "material" (e.g., objects of study) and "methodological" (e.g., methods and models). She also identifies "infrastructural", "socio-cultural" and "institutional" sources of diversity, which have implications for both disciplinary and geographical boundaries. Her analysis relates primarily to questions of inter- and trans-disciplinarity but also hints at broader questions of diversity of epistemic systems or knowledges.

Implicit in many of the critiques of OA we have seen is often a contention that epistemic openness should be extended still further. Such critiques typically argue that all scientific approaches ('science', even broadly conceived) are still essentially Western knowledge systems, and that our understanding of valid and valuable knowledge needs to be extended to encompass other knowledge systems, including those derived from different indigenous communities, quite apart from Western knowledge (Santos, 2016). Aiming to achieve this is attractive, as it ostensibly helps to respond to the critique of scientific knowledge systems in general and OA in particular as being instances of hermeneutical injustice, where other non-Western kinds of hermeneutical systems or resources are devalued (Fricker, 2007). By incorporating the interpretive resources of different knowledge systems within the boundaries of what we consider valid and valuable knowledge (however difficult to do in practice) we can thus begin to address epistemic injustice.

The kind of epistemic openness for which I am arguing is a means of achieving greater diversity and inclusion in the epistemic domain. It is more than open-mindedness – the disposition of being open to different ideas – although it is not less than that. It is also an openness to different kinds of knowledge and different kinds of knowing. It is openness to different methods and frames of reference used to assemble and analyse data, and different approaches used to construct and interpret knowledge. As with all the key arguments in this book, it is not just an individual or personal orientation but additionally needs to be built into systems and structures. I will go on to talk about the relationship between personal agency and social structures in relation to OA elsewhere, particularly in Chapter 7.

Connell (2007) discusses the relationship between knowledge from the Global South, "Southern theory", and how it relates to "Northern theory", from a social sciences point of view in particular. She states it is "not realistic to imagine the future of world social science as a mosaic of distinct knowledge systems—as a set of indigenous sociologies, indigenous economics, and so on, all functioning independently" (p. 223). We are too connected for that. Rather, she points to the need for a more integrative future, and the need for "a more engaged relationship between knowledge systems" and "a mutual learning process on a planetary scale" (p. 222). Achieving such an ambition is an enormous challenge, of course, something which she readily acknowledges, and some aspects of which I will go on to discuss.

This raises important questions about different knowledge types and how knowledge is codified in publications or communicated in other ways. In his discussion of knowledge management, Mingers (2008) distinguishes between four types of knowledge: "propositional" (such as, "I know it is raining"), "experiential" ("I know her well"), "performative" ("I know how to read an X-ray") and "epistemological" ("I know what black holes are"). Conventional scientific and other scholarly research has tended to focus on "epistemological" knowledge, although it may involve others. Scholarly communication itself involves a variety of forms of communication, with different levels of formality – from research seminars to journal articles – but has tended to focus on more formal communication, such as peer-reviewed publications (Borgman, 2007). Other knowledge systems may emphasise different knowledge types and communication forms; for example, some indigenous knowledges may emphasise experiential knowledge communicated in predominantly oral form (Ogone, 2017; UNESCO, 2021). They may also have notions of ownership and stewardship of knowledge different from Western traditions of intellectual property and data protection (Nakata, 2002). Those differences mean that engagement between knowledge systems can be challenging and sensitive. Epistemic openness is difficult to enact in practice, however positive and well-meaning we may be about it in principle.

The concept of "situated openness" is relevant here (Traynor et al., 2019). "Situated openness" is based on the understanding that knowledge is situated and that the approach to openness should be implemented in a way that takes account of the situatedness of the knowledge and the knowledge-generating people and communities involved. Interestingly, the concept has been used as the basis for the argument that there may be grounds for not sharing certain kinds of knowledge openly: for example, to avoid the knowledge being misunderstood or misused, and prevent those generating the knowledge from being inappropriately separated from it or exploited (Albornoz et al., 2019). It is important to note that the argument for epistemic openness should not be taken as an argument that all knowledge should necessarily be shared, any more than the argument for open access or open science should be taken to mean that all outputs of science should always be shared. There are good reasons for not sharing knowledge: personal privacy or commercial confidentiality are often quoted examples. Exploitative appropriation and misuse should be added to the list of reasons for not sharing.

However, the combination of these two words in a single label, "situated openness" creates a tension. Situatedness implies localism, whereas openness implies universality. Making knowledge universally available (openness) necessarily involves removing it from its original local context (situatedness). 'Situated' refers to the knowledge, whereas 'openness' refers to sharing it. Openness itself is not situated, it cannot be, even when knowledge is. This gives the term situated openness a paradoxical character. It also raises a key question: if knowledge is situated, does removing it from its original context to make it open necessarily create negative consequences for the knowledge or its generators? In their study of open data sharing from a situational perspective, Bezuidenhout et al. (2017) emphasise the need to move beyond a focus on "simply making resources available" to one of "fostering researchers' ability to use them". Doing so, arguably enables a kind of re-contextualisation to take place, encouraging appropriate re-use, even if that is challenging. This connects with the idea of participatory openness we will explore in Chapter 8.

Scientific and indigenous knowledges

Despite the challenges, there are a growing number of fields in the research literature which report fruitful engagement between conventional scientific knowledge and indigenous knowledges from countries and cultures in the Global South (Jessen et al., 2022). Some of these focus on environmental issues, including sustainable management of natural resources (Lam et al., 2020), maintaining biodiversity (Ogar et al., 2020), and sustainable agriculture (Soubry et al., 2020). Albuquerque et al. (2021) present a framework for how "traditional ecological knowledge" can be integrated with academic research and policy-making. They suggest a more integrative approach may help to address environmental problems more successfully – doing so in a way that is more likely to be sustainable and inclusive. Many of these principles have been applied in open science projects in various LMICs (Chan et al., 2019).

In some cases, authors have foregrounded key concepts or traditions from indigenous knowledges in order to avoid indigenous knowledges simply being subsumed by or assimilated into conventional scientific knowledge. Reid et al.'s (2021) engagement with the idea of *Etuaptmumk* ("two-eyed seeing" in the Mi'kmaw language), as part of the consideration of fisheries management in Canada, is an example. "Two-eyed seeing" is described by one of the co-authors, a Mi'kmaw Elder, Albert Marshall, as:

> *learning to see from one eye with the strengths of Indigenous knowledges and ways of knowing, and from the other eye with the strengths of mainstream knowledges and ways of knowing, and to use both these eyes together, for the benefit of all.*
>
> (Reid et al., 2021, p. 245)

Such an approach, the authors argue, enables a co-existence of ideas across different epistemic systems. In doing so, it seems to be pushing back against hermeneutical epistemic injustice, since it, and approaches like it, enable the contribution of the hermeneutical resources of indigenous knowledge systems in knowledge generation alongside conventional science.

In the literature on OA, Raju et al. (2020) use the idea of *Ubuntu* to make the case for a particular approach to OA. *Ubuntu* is a Zulu word associated with communal justice and is used by Raju et al. as a basis for arguing for library-based OA publishing in Africa, which, they suggest, could increase participation in scholarly communication amongst African scholars. They describe this approach as part of a more general movement to reshape the way OA is implemented globally:

> *The Open Access movement … must recapture its social justice and inclusivity imperatives in support of the equitable dissemination of Global South scholarship, including African scholarship. The inclusion of content for and by marginalized researchers is driven by the Ubuntu desire for an egalitarian society.*
>
> (Raju et al., 2020, pp. 61–62)

More controversial perhaps are the fields of medicine and health. In the context of the COVID-19 pandemic, Havemann et al. (2020) argued that indigenous medicine should be considered and tested as part of an African response to the emergency. They are careful to argue that such interactions must be conducted sensitively, observing that African researchers should engage in this: "African researchers are well-placed to continually scrutinize research in these areas to preserve data protection, ethics and respectful re-use of indigenous and traditional knowledge" (Havemann et al., 2020, p. 4). Such "re-use" does raise the question of how it is governed, and also what criteria are used for decision-making around it. Western science has often been criticised as being extractive in practice – appropriating insights from other indigenous knowledge systems without benefiting indigenous communities (Igwe et al., 2022). El-Hani et al. (2022) comment:

Many scholars and activists have become concerned about treatment of ILK [Indigenous and Local Knowledge] as an additional data source that is incorporated into dominant scientific accounts only insofar as it proves useful within academic frameworks and natural resource management.

(El-Hani et al., 2022, p. 296)

Creating governance frameworks to ensure genuine interaction rather than extraction, and mutual benefit rather than appropriation, is crucial, and there are a number of sets of principles and guidelines addressing this challenge, most of which have emerged in the 21st century (Klenk et al., 2017; Neylon, 2019; Tankwanchi et al., 2023). A major open science policy document which incorporates what it calls, "open dialogue with other knowledge systems" is the UNESCO Open Science Recommendation (UNESCO, 2021), which provides some pointers in the direction of required governance approaches. These include the 2001 UNESCO Universal Declaration on Cultural Diversity and the 2007 United Nations Declaration on the Rights of Indigenous Peoples. The details of these approaches need to be worked through in relation to open access, and it seems likely that this will be a feature of the scholarly communication landscape in the third decade of the 21st century, building on important work already undertaken (Chan et al., 2019, 2020). Working on this will, I would suggest, enable us to see how greater OA and epistemic openness can complement each other. Many of the developments I have just described of interactions between conventional science and other epistemic systems can be enabled to work more effectively in the context of OA.

A fundamental question arises from this work and my argument for epistemic openness, however. Where there are inconsistencies between knowledges, how can they be resolved? If, for example, an indigenous knowledge system favoured a practice which was regarded as harmful by Western medicine (or vice versa), how should the apparent incommensurability be addressed? This question is important, and so we will explore it and the general problem of incommensurability between knowledge systems in some detail later (particularly in Chapters 6 and 7), having signposted it here.

The nature of the interaction or engagement between different epistemic systems is clearly complex and challenging, and I will continue to discuss it in the chapters that follow, but what is clear at this stage is that epistemic openness involves a complex set of possibilities of dialogue and exchange. Whether this constitutes an extension of the boundaries of science to embrace new epistemologies, or a dialogue of separate epistemic systems with science, is itself a related and contentious point. El-Hani and Souza De Ferreira Bandeira (2008) argue in the context of science education that whilst promoting the value of the interaction between science and indigenous knowledges is important, it is not helpful to bracket indigenous knowledges within 'science', for example, using terminology such as "indigenous science". I find this position persuasive. The best conditions for fruitful engagement between conventional science and indigenous knowledges are most likely to be created, it seems reasonable to suggest, in recognising where there are correspondences between them without trying to gloss over differences. Ludwig and El-Hani (2020) put forward the helpful idea of "partial overlaps" between epistemic systems – where there are "shared ontological, epistemological, or value resources" across systems which provide spaces for interaction and exchange. Such interactions and exchanges are clearly complex, multi-faceted, and dynamic, occurring differently in different areas and times, rather than according to a single settled model. This is particularly the case since indigenous knowledges are themselves highly heterogenous. The phrase 'indigenous knowledges' itself can become problematic, not least because it is used in a way that implies homogeneity where homogeneity does not exist (Battiste & Henderson, 2000). In using shorthand like 'indigenous knowledges' it is important not to lose sight of vast differences between knowledge systems that can render the shorthand highly problematical if used without regard to and respect for such heterogeneity (Agrawal, 1995).

Here we have reached an important point in my argument in relation to global OA. We are moving towards the position that, even if difficult to achieve in practice, a key step we need to take involves extending the boundaries of what is considered valid and valuable knowledge more widely to include other knowledge forms, including non-Western indigenous knowledges. It sounds simple but, as we have begun to see, it is not easy in practice. That recognition leads to a crucial question bound up in the case for epistemic openness: can the move to bring Western science into conversation with other knowledge systems be made to work in a way that is not oppressive, or will conventional science always tend to dominate and marginalise other knowledges? In the next chapter, we will explore different perspectives on this key question as they relate to global OA.

References

Agrawal, A. (1995). Dismantling the divide between indigenous and scientific knowledge. *Development and Change, 26*(3), 413–439. 10.1111/j.1467-7660.1995.tb00560.x. Preprint: https://hdl.handle.net/10535/4201

Albornoz, D., Hillyer, B., Posada, A., Okune, A., & Chan, L. (2019). Principles for an inclusive open science: The OCSNet manifesto. In L. Chan, A. Ratanawaraha, C.

Neylon, H. Vessuri, & H. Thorsteinsdottir (Eds.), *Contextualizing openness: Situating open science* (pp. 23–50). University of Ottowa Press. https://ruor. uottawa.ca/handle/10393/39849

Albuquerque, U. P., Ludwig, D., Feitosa, I. S., de Moura, J. M. B., Gonçalves, P. H. S., da Silva, R. H., da Silva, T. C., Gonçalves-Souza, T., & Ferreira Júnior, W. S. (2021). Integrating traditional ecological knowledge into academic research at local and global scales. *Regional Environmental Change, 21*(2), 45. 10.1007/s10113-021-01774-2

Battiste, M., & Henderson, J. Y. (Sa'ke'j). (2000). *Protecting indigenous knowledge and heritage: A global challenge*. University of British Columbia Press. 10.5 9962/9781895830439

Becher, T., & Trowler, P. (2001). *Academic tribes and territories: Intellectual enquiry and the culture of disciplines (2nd ed.)*. Open University Press.

Berger, P., & Luckmann, T. (1966). *The social construction of reality: A treatise on the sociology of knowledge*. Anchor books.

Bezuidenhout, L. M., Leonelli, S., Kelly, A. H., & Rappert, B. (2017). Beyond the digital divide: Towards a situated approach to open data. *Science and Public Policy, 44*(4), 464–475. 10.1093/scipol/scw036

Borgman, C. L. (2007). *Scholarship in the digital age: Information, infrastructure, and the internet*. MIT Press.

Burr, V. (2015). *Social constructionism (3rd ed.)*. Routledge. 10.4324/9781315 715421

Chan, L., Hall, B., Piron, F., Tandon, R., & Williams, L. (2020). *Open science beyond open access: For and with communities: A step towards the decolonization of knowledge: Prepared for the Canadian Commission for UNESCO*. https://en.ccunesco.ca/-/media/Files/Unesco/Resources/2020/07/ OpenScienceDecolonizingKnowledge.pdf

Chan, L., Ratanawaraha, A., Neylon, C., Vessuri, H., & Thorsteinsdottir, H. (Eds.). (2019). *Contextualizing openness: Situating open science*. University of Ottowa Press. https://ruor.uottawa.ca/handle/10393/39849

Connell, R. (2007). *Southern theory: The global dynamics of knowledge in social science*. Polity.

Elder-Vass, D. (2012). *The reality of social construction*. Cambridge University Press.

El-Hani, C. N., Poliseli, L., & Ludwig, D. (2022). Beyond the divide between indigenous and academic knowledge: Causal and mechanistic explanations in a Brazilian fishing community. *Studies in History and Philosophy of Science, 91*, 296–306. 10.1016/j.shpsa.2021.11.001

El-Hani, C. N., & Souza De Ferreira Bandeira, F. P. (2008). Valuing indigenous knowledge: To call it "science" will not help. *Cultural Studies of Science Education, 3*(3), 751–779. 10.1007/s11422-008-9129-6

Elliott, K. C. (2022). *Values in science*. Cambridge University Press. 10.1017/9781 009052597

Fricker, M. (2007). *Epistemic injustice: Power and the ethics of knowing*. Oxford University Press.

Gerson, E. M. (2013). Integration of specialties: An institutional and organizational view. *Studies in History and Philosophy of Science Part C: Studies in History and Philosophy of Biological and Biomedical Sciences, 44*(4, Part A), 515–524. 10.1016/j.shpsc.2012.10.002

Havemann, J., Bezuidenhout, L., Achampong, J., Akligoh, H., Ayodele, O., Hussein, S., Ksibi, N., Mboa Nkoudou, T. H., Obanda, J., Owango, J., Sanga, V. L., Stirling, J., & Wenzelmann, V. (2020). *Harnessing the open science infrastructure for an efficient African response to COVID-19*. Zenodo. 10.5281/ZENODO.3733768

Igwe, P. A., Madichie, N. O., & Rugara, D. G. (2022). Decolonising research approaches towards non-extractive research. *Qualitative Market Research: An International Journal, 25*(4), 453–468. 10.1108/QMR-11-2021-0135

Jessen, T. D., Ban, N. C., Claxton, N. X., & Darimont, C. T. (2022). Contributions of indigenous knowledge to ecological and evolutionary understanding. *Frontiers in Ecology and the Environment, 20*(2), 93–101. 10.1002/fee.2435

Kagan, J. (2009). *The three cultures: Natural sciences, social sciences, and the humanities in the 21st century*. Cambridge University Press.

Klenk, N., Fiume, A., Meehan, K., & Gibbes, C. (2017). Local knowledge in climate adaptation research: Moving knowledge frameworks from extraction to co-production. *WIREs Climate Change, 8*(5), e475. 10.1002/wcc.475

Kukla, A. (2000). *Social constructivism and the philosophy of science*. Psychology Press.

Lam, D. P. M., Hinz, E., Lang, D., Tengö, M., Wehrden, H., & Martín-López, B. (2020). Indigenous and local knowledge in sustainability transformations research: A literature review. *Ecology and Society, 25*(1), 3. 10.5751/ES-11305-250103

Leonelli, S. (2022). Open science and epistemic diversity: Friends or foes? *Philosophy of Science, 89*(5), 991–1001. 10.1017/psa.2022.45

Lincoln, Y. S., & Guba, E. G. (2016). *The constructivist credo*. Routledge. 10.4324/9781315418810

Ludwig, D., & El-Hani, C. N. (2020). Philosophy of ethnobiology: Understanding knowledge integration and its limitations. *Journal of Ethnobiology, 40*(1), 3–20. 10.2993/0278-0771-40.1.3

McKaughan, D. J. (2008). From ugly duckling to swan: C. S. Peirce, abduction, and the pursuit of scientific theories. *Transactions of the Charles S. Peirce Society, 44*(3), 446–468. https://www.jstor.org/stable/40321321

McMullin, E. (1992). *The inference that makes science*. Marquette University Press.

Mingers, J. (2008). Management knowledge and knowledge management: Realism and forms of truth. *Knowledge Management Research & Practice, 6*(1), 62–76. 10.1057/palgrave.kmrp.8500161

Nakata, M. (2002). Indigenous knowledge and the cultural interface: Underlying issues at the intersection of knowledge and information systems. *IFLA Journal, 28*(5–6), 281–291. 10.1177/034003520202800513

Neylon, C. (2019). Governing open science: Introduction. In L. Chan, A. Ratanawaraha, C. Neylon, H. Vessuri, & H. Thorsteinsdottir (Eds.), *Contextualizing openness: Situating open science* (pp. 125–132). University of Ottowa Press. https://ruor.uottawa.ca/handle/10393/39849

Ogar, E., Pecl, G., & Mustonen, T. (2020). Science must embrace traditional and indigenous knowledge to solve our biodiversity crisis. *One Earth, 3*(2), 162–165. 10.1016/j.oneear.2020.07.006

Ogone, J. O. (2017). Epistemic injustice: African knowledge and scholarship in the global context. In A. Bartels, L. Eckstein, N. Waller, & D. Wiemann (Eds.), *Postcolonial Justice* (Vol. 191, pp. 17–36). Brill Leiden. 10.1163/9789004335196_004

Oreskes, N. (2019). *Why trust science?* Princeton University Press.

Potter, J. (1996). *Representing reality*. Sage Publications. http://www.myilibrary.com?id=255907

Raju, R., Claassen, J., Madini, N., Suliaman, T., & Nowviskie, B. (2020). Social justice and inclusivity: Drivers for the dissemination of African scholarship. In M. P. Eve, & J. Gray (Eds.), *Reassembling Scholarly Communications* (pp. 53–64). The MIT Press. 10.7551/mitpress/11885.003.0008

Reid, A. J., Eckert, L. E., Lane, J.-F., Young, N., Hinch, S. G., Darimont, C. T., Cooke, S. J., Ban, N. C., & Marshall, A. (2021). "Two-eyed seeing": An indigenous framework to transform fisheries research and management. *Fish and Fisheries, 22*(2), 243–261. 10.1111/faf.12516

Rivas, J. (2010). Realism. For real this time: Scientific realism is not a compromise between positivism and interpretivism. In J. Joseph, & C. Wight (Eds.), *Scientific Realism and International Relations* (pp. 203–227). Palgrave Macmillan. 10.1057/9780230281981_12

Santos, B. de S. (2016). *Epistemologies of the South: Justice against epistemicide.* Routledge.

Sayer, A. (2010). Reductionism in social science. In R. E. Lee (Ed.), *Questioning nineteenth-century assumptions about knowledge, II: Reductionism* (pp. 5–39). State University of New York Press. https://sunypress.edu/Books/Q/Questioning-Nineteenth-Century-Assumptions-about-Knowledge-II

Sayer, A. (2012). Power, causality and normativity: A critical realist critique of Foucault. *Journal of Political Power, 5*(2), 179–194. 10.1080/2158379X.2012.698898

Sorell, T. (1994). *Scientism: Philosophy and the infatuation with science.* Routledge. https://www.routledge.com/Scientism-Philosophy-and-the-Infatuation-with-Science/Sorell/p/book/9780415107716

Soubry, B., Sherren, K., & Thornton, T. F. (2020). Are we taking farmers seriously? A review of the literature on farmer perceptions and climate change, 2007–2018. *Journal of Rural Studies, 74*, 210–222. 10.1016/j.jrurstud.2019.09.005

Tankwanchi, A. S., Asabor, E. N., & Vermund, S. H. (2023). Global health perspectives on race in research: Neocolonial extraction and local marginalization. *International Journal of Environmental Research and Public Health, 20*(13), Article 13. 10.3390/ijerph20136210

Traynor, C., Foster, L., & Schonwetter, T. (2019). Tensions related to openness in researching indigenous peoples' knowledge systems and intellectual property rights. In L. Chan, A. Ratanawaraha, C. Neylon, H. Vessuri, & H. Thorsteinsdottir (Eds.), *Contextualizing openness: Situating open science* (pp. 223–236). University of Ottowa Press. https://ruor.uottawa.ca/handle/10393/39849

Trowler, P., Saunders, M., & Bamber, V. (Eds.). (2012). *Tribes and territories in the 21st century: Rethinking the significance of disciplines in higher education.* Routledge.

UNESCO. (2021). *UNESCO recommendation on open science.* UNESCO. https://unesdoc.unesco.org/ark:/48223/pf0000379949.locale=en

Vienni-Baptista, B., Fletcher, I., Lyall, C., & Pohl, C. (2022). Embracing heterogeneity: Why plural understandings strengthen interdisciplinarity and transdisciplinarity. *Science and Public Policy, 49*(6), 865–877. 10.1093/scipol/scac034

5   Epistemic openness and knowledge-based oppression

There are two major issues that need discussing in relation to the argument, outlined in the previous chapter, for epistemic openness – the widening of our epistemic boundaries – as a complement to scientific openness. The two issues come from different theoretical directions. First, there is the contention that knowledge is a vehicle for epistemic/cognitive oppression. Second, there is the problem of the incommensurability of knowledges. We have already had glimpses of both, but they both need more focused discussion in relation to the case for epistemic openness and its relationship with OA. We need to cover theory as well as tease out practical implications. I will discuss the first issue in this chapter. The second, I will introduce in the latter part of this chapter and then go on to discuss it further in the chapter that follows. I am going to make the case that what I will call 'softer' versions of the argument for knowledge as a vehicle for epistemic oppression involve a 'moderate constructionism', and I will relate these to the idea of bias. Addressing biases of various sorts is a significant priority for science in general, including the domain of scholarly communication. However, I will argue, 'harder' versions of the epistemic oppression narrative rely on 'thoroughgoing constructionism' and, I will contend, create problems. There are particular problems of relativism and incommensurability, which help to indicate where the limits of the argument for epistemic openness should lie.

The challenge of bias

I want to argue that there are 'softer' and 'harder' versions of the idea that knowledge is a form of epistemic/cognitive oppression. The softer version is most often seen in terms like 'bias' and emphasises that systems and approaches around knowledge generation are inequitable and therefore disadvantage certain groups, biasing knowledge itself. Onie (2020), for example, observes:

> More than 75% of articles analysed in a survey of the journal
> Psychological Science drew participant samples from Western

DOI: 10.4324/9781032679259-5

countries, despite these countries contributing just 12% to the global population … . Such bias affects our understanding of the natural world, and makes it more difficult for researchers from parts of Asia, Africa and Latin America to operate effectively.

(Onie, 2020, p. 37)

Onie identifies two problems here. The first problem is that "bias affects our understanding of the natural world" – an epistemic problem. The second problem is that it is "more difficult for researchers from parts of Asia, Africa and Latin America to operate effectively" – a participatory problem. It is these two problems that I am proposing need to be addressed by epistemic openness and participatory openness, respectively. I will come to the second later (in Chapter 8 particularly); but with regard to the first, it is clear that fundamental change needs to happen in the way science is conducted. A similar point, again relating to psychology, is made by Adetula et al. (2022), arguing a common approach in the discipline is to "almost universally investigate whether effects discovered in North America or Europe generalize to other populations", not the other way round. This kind of approach is not unique to psychology. It applies to a greater or lesser extent to all disciplines. It clearly needs to be addressed by placing more emphasis on generating findings amongst other populations or in other contexts, including in LMICs, and tested in other directions. Here then the knowledge we have is biased because of the way it is constructed, and we need to address this problem in ways that are relevant for the different disciplines concerned.

Other examples of such Eurocentrism (or Western- or Northern-centrism) and similar particularism are associated with subjects of study and theories. On the first issue of the subjects of study, an important example would be where health research focuses on Western priorities, such as health conditions prevalent in HICs, rather than those predominantly affecting LMICs (Yegros-Yegros et al., 2020). In the humanities, the prevalence of European literature in literary and cultural research, particularly literature in English, is a common form of bias (Blasi et al., 2022). On the question of theory, the preponderance of social, economic, or political theories generated from European thought, many of which are simply assumed to be universally applicable, is also evidence of bias. Even in fields with purportedly global reach, such as international relations, Noda (2020) shows how concepts and foci in the field are often Western-centric, which is reflected in the journals that are dominant in international relations.

Despite such problems, Onie (2020) makes the point that openness itself can help address the challenges, by, for instance, exposing biases and creating an environment in which they can be addressed. Addressing biases creates a challenging agenda for the research community in general and the OA community in particular, of course, but OA itself may be part of the solution. Scientific openness can expose bias, and ensure it is subject to scrutiny and critique, making it more likely that different perspectives are brought to bear on issues, something I will discuss later, in Chapter 8. The fact that knowledge is constructed and situated means that bringing different perspectives to bear on an issue can help to create a more rounded understanding of an issue and can reduce the impact of biases. This approach might be called 'moderately constructionist' since it relies on there being an ontological reality independent of our perceptions, but at the same time, recognises that knowledge about reality is constructed from particular perspectives and in particular situations. We shall go on to talk about the moderately constructionist approach in more detail in Chapter 7.

However, it is important to recognise that the concept of bias has come under criticism. Inherent in the idea of epistemic bias seems to be the assumption that a normative position can be reached when biases are removed – a kind of objective even keel (Lee et al., 2013). Many constructionists would argue that objectivity in knowledge cannot in fact be achieved, even though the drive to eliminate biases implies it can. Some might argue that this means the concept of bias is invalid and it should not be used at all. An alternative to that argument would involve the acknowledgement that whilst knowledge is always constructed and depends on the perspective of the knower, it is possible that unfairness relating to different perspectives may still be reduced (Hammersley & Gomm, 1997). If bias is "unwarranted prejudice" (Buetow & Zawaly, 2022) or unfair pre-judgement, then there may be some approaches that can reduce such problems, or at least make them more transparent.

At the centre of this disagreement about the language of bias is the question of whether underlying our knowledge is an objective reality that can be discerned, even if imperfectly, or whether the understanding that knowledge is constructed precludes ideas like bias. Does recognising the constructedness of knowledge allow for an underlying notion of normativity or do we have to relinquish any idea of normativity and then work with an entirely relativistic framework within and between knowledge systems? Put another way, are there limits to constructionism and if so, where are they located? That is something we now need to go on to explore through the idea of knowledge and power and its relation to OA debates.

Knowledge and power

The objection to the idea of bias, or at least, the possibility of objectivity that the idea of bias implies, leads us to consider harder forms of the argument that knowledge is a vehicle for epistemic/cognitive oppression. Harder forms of the argument are often based on more thoroughgoing constructionist meta-theory. Such arguments have been put forward by critics of OA, or at least, they have co-opted social theory which relies on thoroughly constructionist meta-theory. Such a position is, I believe, difficult to reconcile with support for OA. We need, therefore, to spend more time unpacking the arguments and showing how they relate to epistemic openness and OA.

The harder arguments tend to be based on theory that emphasises the importance of the relationship between knowledge and power. Gramsci's theory of 'hegemony' is foundational (Gramsci, 1937). The theory developed by Gramsci, working along similar lines as members of the Frankfurt School of Critical Theory (Gordon et al., 2018), contributed to an important strand of neo-Marxist social analysis from the 1920s onwards. The work was focused on a major quandary arising from Marxian thought: how had mature capitalist societies perpetuated themselves without collapsing (Stoddart, 2007)? Marx had predicted that such societies would crumble under the weight of capitalism's own internal contradictions and be swept away by revolution (Marx, 1887). However, the most advanced capitalist societies (which Marx predicted would be the first to collapse), had in fact reformed themselves by reducing economic inequalities and extending political participation. This needed explaining. It was in response to this conundrum that the theory of hegemonic power was developed.

Power invested in elites, it was proposed, was exercised not merely through economic and coercive means, but also cultural institutions and forms of knowledge, through which the 'consent' of the population as a whole for the status quo could be achieved, despite socio-economic inequalities. The development of class consciousness, an important precursor to revolution, could be dampened down through these dominant knowledge systems and cultural institutions. This was a development of Marx's ideas of 'ideology', by which the economically dominant maintained their power. Significantly, however, it widened the importance of ideas, seeing them as structurally important, holding in place existing power relationships (Stoddart, 2007). The significant influence of the mass media, something which fascinated many Critical Theorists of the Frankfurt School, was part of this social structure. The key ideas involved were wrapped up in the term 'hegemony', as used by Gramsci in particular (Bates, 1975; Femia, 1975). The idea that social equality and authentic democracy could be achieved through parliamentary elections was seen by Gramsci as one of the most successful "ideological bluffs" of capitalist societies, a scepticism shared by other critical theorists as evidence of cultural hegemony (Gramsci, 1978).

Although the idea of hegemonic power was originally developed within a realist paradigm, its emphasis on knowledge as a construction, and the link between knowledge and power, meant that it adumbrated many of the aspects of the constructionist paradigm that was to follow. Since the 1960s, ideas such as hegemony have often been deployed within a thoroughly constructionist framework. The use of the concept was influenced by early postmodern theory, particularly theory developed by poststructuralists like Foucault, who regarded power as the overridingly important factor through which social relations could be properly understood (Best & Kellner, 1997). Power was present in a complex web of social relationships and interactions, and was maintained through "discourses", ways of seeing and talking about the world that establish and reinforce our understandings of reality, and social and behavioural norms (Foucault, 1977a). In this way, discourses are defined by Foucault as "practices which form the objects of which they speak" (Foucault, 1972, p. 49) – discourses make reality. The construction of knowledge (including scientific knowledge), and the perception of reality that derives from it, reinforce structures of power, an idea Foucault captures in the term, "power/knowledge" (Foucault, 1967, 1977b, 1980). Any truth claims (including those of science) are socially contingent: "Every society has its regime of truth, its 'general politics'of truth: that is, the types of discourse which it accepts and makes function as true" (Foucault, 1980, p. 131).

Much postcolonial theory interacts with these ideas about power, applying them in the context of coloniality. Hegemonic power is seen as being exercised by Western former colonial countries, who achieve dominance in a number of ways, not least through knowledge systems. The Gramscian term, "subaltern", is used to describe indigenous peoples who are excluded from power through colonialism and neo-colonial hegemonic systems, particularly alien epistemologies (Spivak, 1988). In what is often seen as one of the founding texts of postmodern postcolonial theory, *Orientalism,* Edward Said (1979) explicitly frames his analysis by combining Gramsci's theory of hegemony and Foucault's idea of discourse, and their association of knowledge and power, to make his case about the way in which an understanding of the "other" was constructed in the West with regard to the "Orient", enabling Western countries to dominate non-Western ones (Said, 1979). Said's work has often been cited as influential by subsequent postcolonial scholars, including those working outside literary studies (Connell, 2007).

Goodwin-Smith (2010) explains the relationship between Foucault and Gramsci in Said's thought:

> *Said uses a marriage of Foucault to Gramsci in his investigation of the narratives of identity. He suggests that hegemony is formed discursively – that a Gramscian hegemony of knowing, a cultural way of life, or a community of consensus and common sense, is established discursively, or*

textually, in a manner which can be understood in terms of Foucault. As formative agents of a Gramscian consensual hegemony, Said views textuality and discourse in a Foucauldian sense, as colonising technologies of knowledge and power.

(Goodwin-Smith, 2010, p. 592)

Following Said, the argument at the core of many postcolonial studies has been that neo-colonial domination involves not merely economic exploitation, but also epistemic oppression of indigenous peoples, with Western knowledge used to side-line other epistemologies (Santos, 2018). Spivak's (1988) notion of "epistemic violence" has been particularly influential in framing this discourse (Brunner, 2021). Even after Western powers divested themselves of their empires, epistemic domination of indigenous peoples in LMICs continued, and still requires "epistemic decolonization" (Nhemachena et al., 2020; Posholi, 2020). The epistemic decolonisation argument often draws on (explicitly or implicitly) the combination of Gramscian theory of hegemony and Foucauldian theory of power/knowledge, following Said and others.

Whether the "marriage of Foucault to Gramsci" is an entirely happy one is a moot point. Such a close association of the Gramscian hegemony theory and Foucauldian power/knowledge theory in Said's thought, and much postcolonial literature that has followed, is contro-versial. Said's approach has been criticised for attempting to combine what are often seen as different theories of power (Day, 2005; Geras, 1990). Gramsci's macro-social top-down notion of hegemonic power is often seen as fundamentally different from Foucault's micro-social knowledge/power networks. Foucault's analysis of power notably did not deal in any detail with colonial power – Young (1995) goes so far as calling Foucault's thought "scrupulously Eurocentric" (p. 57). However, others have made the case for the fundamental complementarity of the theories (Kreps, 2016). Stoddart's (2007) picture of Gramscian notions of hegemony and Foucauldian power/knowledge as being at different points of the same continuum of ideas of power – which combine notions of knowledge, discourse and identity in different ways – is helpful for understanding many accounts of postcolonial theory which often implicitly combine elements of the two, albeit taking up different positions on that continuum. That is not to say that postcolonial studies systematically reconcile these theories in a way that has created consensus, but rather that they often draw on both (albeit in different ways and with different emphases) to inform their analyses, along with others including postmodern theorists, such as Derrida and activist scholars, such as Fanon (Prakash, 1994; Rattansi, 1997).

An important aspect of the argument for epistemic oppression is the relativising of Western scientific knowledge. Nanda (2001) has commented on the large number of social and cultural theorists who "have demanded 'epistemic parity' between modern science and other knowledge-traditions" (p. 167). In making such demands, particular attention is usually given to the situatedness of knowledge and consequently "positionality" (Haraway, 1988). Ideas of the epistemological importance of standpoint and positionality were first developed within feminist theory, and because of the close association of some strands of feminist theory with postcolonial theory, have been elaborated within postcolonial narratives (Harding, 1998, 2006). Within this frame, all epistemologies are situated and contingent, associated with particular peoples in particular contexts. Western science is one such situated epistemic system (Santos, 2016). 'Lived experience', therefore, becomes crucial in knowledge – epistemic insight depends on the positionality, and therefore, standpoint of the knower (Harding, 2015).

Many of the elements of this harder version of the knowledge-as-oppression argument seem to be evident in critiques of OA, influenced as they are by critical and postcolonial thought. In particular, Gramscian and Foucauldian concepts are commonly used, as we have seen in the work of Knöchelmann (2021) and Piron (2018), particularly notions of hegemony and discourse, and their association with Western science. There is also often an emphasis on the situatedness of scientific knowledge and on the positionality of the knower, including Piron's argument already seen for an "African science". The idea of "situated openness", applied in open science, generally explicitly draws on feminist and postcolonial critique (Traynor et al., 2019). Haider (2007) refers to the "hegemonic discourses" used to support arguments for OA, at the centre of which is the "view of science as a neutral, privileged, and crucially as a universal form of knowledge" (p. 456), a view which she questions. Knöchelmann's arguments regarding hermeneutical injustice make the use of these conceptual frames clear:

> Essentially, then, in the sense of a globalised production of knowledge, non-Global North scholars are treated unjust [sic] in that they contribute far less to global hermeneutic resources, or their modes of contribution are disturbed by the Northern-influenced global discourse. Moreover, especially within a Global North hegemony, clusters of epistemes are often artificially specialised and outsourced which renders their idiosyncrasies as another *preemptively:* race studies, indigenous studies, or gender studies are but a few examples here.
>
> (Knöchelmann, 2021, p. 77, emphasis original)

The use of ideas of 'hegemony', 'epistemes' and implicitly the idea of standpoint (in 'anothering') are all important reflections of this theoretical heritage. Although Haider, Knöchelmann, Piron and others support OA, albeit in a radically changed form, there are few explicit attempts to reconcile their co-opting of these concepts based on (often thorough-going) constructionist meta-theory with support for OA, when support for OA, as we have seen, assumes the universal value of scientific outputs, at least in some sense.

Problems with thoroughgoing constructionism

The social theories that give rise to the harder versions of the knowledge-as-oppression argument are built on a thoroughgoing constructionism. I want to argue that this foundation is shaky. In doing so, I will refer to a range of thinkers but will treat Foucauldian analysis, and how it has been critiqued, as a kind of reference point. Foucault's thought is particularly influential, and so focusing on his approach is a pragmatic way of navigating the key issues without completely disappearing down an epistemic rabbit hole.

The ideas of constructionists are framed in different ways, of course, but a key claim often made is summarised by Burr (2015), arguing a constructionist case: "Social constructionism is not claiming that language and discourse merely have a strong influence upon our perception of reality. What we know as reality is itself a construction" (p. 92). Smith (2010), defines what he calls "strong constructionism" in the following way:

> *Reality itself for humans is a human, social construction, constituted by human mental categories, discursive practices, definitions of situations, and symbolic exchanges that are sustained as 'real' through ongoing social interactions that are in turn shaped by particular interests, perspectives, and, usually, imbalances of power – our knowledge about reality is therefore entirely culturally relative, since no human has access to reality 'as it really is' (if such a thing exists or can be talked about intelligibly) because we can never escape our human epistemo-logical and linguistic limits to verify whether our beliefs about reality correspond with externally objective reality.*
>
> (Smith, 2010, p. 122)

I have said that such constructionism is a shaky foundation for social theory. However, before we can consider its shakiness, we first need to contend with the slipperiness of the concepts in this area. It is often difficult to come to a fixed idea of what some constructionists are actually claiming. For instance, Burr's statement that "what we know as reality is itself a construction" could be read in a number of ways: as a statement about our perceptions (epistemology) or the world (ontology) or some kind of combination of the two (Elder-Vass, 2012). Any exploration of this area will quickly meet the challenge of trying to ascertain the ontological and epistemological foundations of social theory based on thoroughgoing constructionism. Many thoroughgoing constructionists have a tendency to foreground knowledge and epistemology, but in doing so, occlude questions of ontology (Elder-Vass, 2012). It is often difficult to ascertain the ontology implicit in many constructionists' work. This is complicated by what Smith (2010) calls "slippage" in many constructionist accounts. At times, some constructionist studies may make moderately constructionist claims about social influences on our understanding of reality, but also slide into making more radical claims about the 'world' or 'reality' as constructions, without being clear this is happening. Smith observes, "such ambiguities and slippery connotations seem to allow writers to pitch various edgy social, epistemological, and ontological claims while leaving open an escape door of plausible deniability in case anyone detects strong constructionism lurking" (Smith, 2010, p. 126).

The tendency to foreground knowledge and epistemology is evident in Foucault's thought. Burr (2015) defines Foucault's approach in these terms:

> *He does not deny the materiality of events, but says that our only way of apprehending reality is through discourse, which determines our perceptions of reality. In a sense, Foucault brackets off the question of reality. Since we can never have direct access to a reality beyond discourse we cannot concern ourselves with its nature.*
>
> (Burr, 2015, p. 103)

This 'bracketing off' of questions of reality in Foucault's writing is a common feature of constructionist work. Reality (in so far as we can talk about a reality beyond our perceptions) is not accessible to us in any kind of 'raw' state but is only apprehensible through language and discourse, which themselves shape our reality. Often this seems to involve a collapsing of ontology into epistemology, resulting in a constructed whole – in which reality and knowledge of reality become conflated. Although there have been attempts to present Foucault as a realist (Pearce & Woodiwiss, 2001), his insistence on our ability to perceive reality only through discourse, his emphasis on knowledge as always strongly situated, and his resistance to any totalising explanations, dominate his writings and militate against placing him within a realist paradigm. Joseph (2004) presents a measured account of Foucault's notions of reality, which does something to pull Foucault's thought into more realist terrain, but he still observes:

> *Foucault's work does contain an irrealist impulse, which is to stake his all on the transitive domain of knowledge, and to define reality*

according to the power of discourses or the Nietzschean struggles of power-knowledge. There is a tendency in Foucault to reduce truth-claims to rhetorical narrative strategies.

(Joseph, 2004, p. 145)

Joseph's observation about power is crucial here. The construction of knowledge, any understanding of reality, is said to be based on social factors, most notably, power (Foucault, 1997). Amongst thoroughgoing constructionists, analysis of social systems often becomes a search for power relations in those systems, and understanding knowledge itself as socially constructed becomes an analysis of how it is related to power. Foucault (1977a) goes so far as to claim that "in fact, power produces; it produces reality; it produces domains of objects and rituals of truth" (p. 194).

Elder-Vass (2012) spells out the implications of the argument "offered by Michel Foucault", and adopted by many others, "that all knowledge represents an exercise of power":

This gives us what I will call social determination of meaning*: the claim that the meanings we associate with linguistic terms and structures are not fixed by reference to the world, but as the outcome of social power battles. This in turn leads to the conclusion that there is no way to ground language (and hence knowledge expressed through language) objectively in the world. Instead, according to extreme linguistic constructionists, our conceptions of the world are determined by power through the medium of language. Hence the argument leads to* strong epistemic relativism*: We must become relativists about all knowledge claims, because if our very concepts are the product of power and can only be altered by the operation of competing powers, there can be no objective basis on which to judge that any one claim about the world is better founded than any other.*

(Elder-Vass, 2012, p. 78, emphasis original)

Distinguishing between different constructions in knowledge, therefore, becomes arbitrary, depending on the power of their proponents. As Taylor (1984) has pointed out, according to this position, any truth claims are merely substituting one "regime of truth" for another, simply based on their relative power. Taylor emphasises that one consequence of this is that any ethical claim cannot have normative grounding; instead, an ethical position itself becomes a power play. Consistent with this, Foucauldian accounts often avoid judgements on whether certain forms of power are good or bad, although, interestingly, his analysis, at the same time, often has undercurrents of ethical judgements which are never fully surfaced (Habermas, 1986; Taylor, 1984). Such an approach has been criticised as "crypto-normative" (Sayer, 2012). Regardless, we are left with a profound moral relativism (Smith, 2010), which creates massive individual and societal dilemmas. For example, Miroslav Volf has pointed out the inability of a Foucauldian approach to knowledge and truth to allow a 'truth and reconciliation' process following conflict (Volf, 2019). Such a process requires a mutual understanding of events that actually happened, and acceptance of a normative ethical framework, in order to effect any reconciliation – epistemic and moral resources that a Foucauldian approach cannot provide.

But the problems go deeper still. The thoroughgoing constructionist position is ultimately epistemologically self-defeating. Elder-Vass again:

> *Foucault was a major source of one of the most pervasive and persuasive tendencies in late twentieth-century social theory: the tendency to challenge conventional assumptions about knowledge by exposing the dependence of knowledge claims on unacknowledged social influences. Such critiques have often been taken as undermining the reliability of knowledge claims in general; yet they are knowledge claims themselves, and it remains unclear whether and how they might attain some kind of reflexive equilibrium in which they contribute productively to our understanding of knowledge without undermining their own epistemic status.*
>
> (Elder-Vass, 2012, p. 207)

Putting it simply, if any knowledge claim is dependent on social influences, which apparently undermines its reliability, then the knowledge claim that any knowledge claim is based on social influences is *itself* also based on social influences, also undermining *its* reliability. Then in turn *that* knowledge claim is based on social influences, again undermining its own reliability. And so on, *ad infinitum*. The thoroughgoing constructionist position, therefore, creates an infinite regress in which any knowledge claims are self-undermining.

Smith (2010) spells out the consequences of thoroughgoing or "strong" constructionism:

> *... if the strong version is actually right, there is no reason to take it seriously, because then it would be only one of many possible culturally relative constructions of knowledge about 'reality,' the merits of which we have no reliable independent standard by which to judge. Someone may wish to believe it or not for personal, aesthetic, or purely arbitrary reasons, but, in any case, by its own account it would offer no rationally coherent reasons with which to compel the agreement of others. Stated in other terms, if social constructionism is correct, then the authority of the social constructionist herself or himself is undermined by her or his own argument ... .*
>
> (Smith, 2010, p. 136)

This gives rise to the question: how is it possible to distinguish between the merits of different knowledge claims within and between knowledge systems in a thoroughgoing constructionist frame? We cannot avoid the conclusion that it is impossible to do so. We have a problem of self-defeating relativism (Groff, 2004). We have no means of distinguishing between different, even incommensurable knowledge claims. Moreover, we can have no ethical basis for adopting activist or interventionist positions, since it is impossible to ground them in a meaningful ethical framework which is based on anything other than the subjectivist perceptions and relative power of its advocates.

For these reasons, I contend that it is difficult to maintain a hard version of the argument that scientific knowledge is a vehicle for epistemic/cognitive injustice, based, as it is, on a thoroughgoing constructionist paradigm, whilst, at the same time, still being a supporter of OA. The hard form of the knowledge-as-oppression argument made in relation to OA in fact undermines the case for OA. If the knowledge being disseminated is a vehicle for power and a form of oppression, then OA itself is a vehicle for power and a form of oppression, since OA makes that knowledge more widely and easily available. In that case, there is no defensible rationale for sharing that knowledge – quite the opposite, declining to share it removes an oppressive force. The softer version of the knowledge-as-oppression argument, with its emphasis on bias in knowledge construction, and itself based on a more moderate form of constructionism (which still acknowledges social influences in constructing knowledge), offers hope in principle of correcting biases, even if doing so is challenging in practice. However, the harder form of the knowledge-as-oppression argument, based on a thoroughgoing constructionism, offers little hope of such a resolution. It also offers no basis for an ethical grounding for action in response to oppression. Knowledge will always be at base a reflection of and vehicle for power, and so will any ethical position put forward to justify action. OA cannot be justified within this theoretical framework, and the co-option of such arguments by critics of OA in fact makes the case for OA irrecoverable.

This analysis leads us to the second major issue arising from the idea of epistemic openness, mentioned at the beginning of this chapter: the incommensurability of knowledges. When different knowledge claims clash, can their apparent incommensurability be resolved, or does the case for epistemic openness inevitably mean irresolvable relativism? It is important to emphasise that different knowledge systems do not always necessarily clash. Different knowledges and different ways of knowing, even ones ostensibly incommensurable, can be complementary, and dialogue between them yields fruitful insights (McGrath, 2019). We saw this earlier when looking at the exchange between scientific and other indigenous knowledges. However, at times, contradictions *will* arise.

To return to a case already mentioned – the case of medicine: if recommended health treatments derived from Western health sciences conflict with approaches favoured in an indigenous knowledge system, how can this conflict be resolved? Where there is a possible medical intervention recommended by clinicians working within the frame of conventional medicine, and a different intervention favoured by another knowledge system, it seems difficult to shrug our epistemic shoulders and say we simply need to live with difference. We are faced with a choice. On what basis might we justify an intervention when different forms of evidence from different and incompatible epistemic systems are available? Incommensurability problems of this sort could arise in a vast range of fields and in relation to a large variety of knowledge claims. For example, there may be different claims about how we best manage environmental systems or how to decide between different ethical positions. How can these conflicts be resolved? Do we need to set limits on how far epistemic openness extends, and if so, where do such limits lie? These are questions that may at times be made more obvious because of open access – because OA makes it easier for different and contradictory claims to be apparent to us. In the next chapter, I want to go on to engage with one major thinker whose ideas tell us a great deal about how different knowledge systems can co-exist and interact, and whose work has significant implications for debates on openness.

References

Adetula, A., Forscher, P. S., Basnight-Brown, D., Azouaghe, S., & IJzerman, H. (2022). Psychology should generalize from—not just to—Africa. *Nature Reviews Psychology, 1*, 370–371. 10.1038/s44159-022-00070-y

Bates, T. R. (1975). Gramsci and the theory of hegemony. *Journal of the History of Ideas, 36*(2), 351–366. 10.2307/2708933

Best, S., & Kellner, D. (1997). *Postmodern theory: Critical interrogations.* Macmillan.

Blasi, D. E., Henrich, J., Adamou, E., Kemmerer, D., & Majid, A. (2022). Over-reliance on English hinders cognitive science. *Trends in Cognitive Sciences, 26*(12), 1153–1170. 10.1016/j.tics.2022.09.015

Brunner, C. (2021). Conceptualizing epistemic violence: An interdisciplinary assemblage for IR. *International Politics Reviews, 9*(1), 193–212. 10.1057/s41312-021-00086-1

Buetow, S., & Zawaly, K. (2022). Rethinking researcher bias in health research. *Journal of Evaluation in Clinical Practice, 28*(5), 843–846. 10.1111/jep.13622

Burr, V. (2015). *Social constructionism (3rd ed.).* Routledge. 10.4324/9781315715421

Connell, R. (2007). *Southern theory: The global dynamics of knowledge in social science.* Polity.

Day, R. J. F. (2005). *Gramsci is dead: Anarchist currents in the newest social movements.* Pluto Press.

Elder-Vass, D. (2012). *The reality of social construction.* Cambridge University Press.
Femia, J. (1975). Hegemony and consciousness in the thought of Antonio Gramsci. *Political Studies, 23*(1), 29–48. 10.1111/j.1467-9248.1975.tb00044.x
Foucault, M. (1967). *Madness and civilization: A history of insanity in the age of reason (R. Howard, Trans.).* Tavistock.
Foucault, M. (1972). *The archaeology of knowledge.* Tavistock Publications.
Foucault, M. (1977a). *Discipline and punish: The birth of the prison (1st American ed.).* Pantheon Books.
Foucault, M. (1977b). *The history of sexuality. Vol. 1: An introduction.* Penguin Books.
Foucault, M. (1980). *Power/knowledge: Selected interviews and other writings, 1972-1977 (C. Gordon, Trans.; 1st American ed.).* Pantheon Books.
Foucault, M. (1997). *The politics of truth* (S. Lotringer & L. Hochroth, Eds.). MIT Press.
Geras, N. (1990). *Discourses of extremity: Radical ethics and post-Marxist extravagances.* Verso.
Goodwin-Smith, I. (2010). Resisting Foucault: The necessity of appropriation. *Social Identities, 16*(5), 587–596. 10.1080/13504630.2010.509561
Gordon, P. E., Hammer, E., & Honneth, A. (Eds.). (2018). *The Routledge companion to the Frankfurt school.* Routledge.
Gramsci, A. (1937). *Prison notebooks (J. A. Buttigieg, Ed.; A. Callari, Trans.).* Columbia University Press.
Gramsci, A. (1978). *The modern prince and other writings.* International Publishing.
Groff, R. (2004). *Critical Realism, Post-positivism and the Possibility of Knowledge.* Routledge. 10.4324/9780203417270
Habermas, J. (1986). Taking aim at the heart of the present. In D. C. Hoy (Ed.), *Foucault: A critical reader.* Basil Blackwell.
Haider, J. (2007). Of the rich and the poor and other curious minds: On open access and "development". *Aslib Proceedings, 59*(4/5), 449–461. 10.1108/00012530710817636
Hammersley, M., & Gomm, R. (1997). Bias in social research. *Sociological Research Online, 2*(1), 7–19. 10.5153/sro.55
Haraway, D. (1988). Situated knowledges: The science question in feminism and the privilege of partial perspective. *Feminist Studies, 14*(3), 575–599.
Harding, S. G. (1998). *Is science multicultural? Postcolonialisms, feminisms and epistemologies.* Indiana University Press.
Harding, S. G. (2006). *Science and social inequality: Feminist and postcolonial issues.* University of Illinois Press.
Harding, S. G. (2015). *Objectivity and diversity: Another logic of scientific research.* University of Chicago Press.
Joseph, J. (2004). Foucault and reality. *Capital & Class, 28*(1), 143–165. 10.1177/030981680408200108
Knöchelmann, M. (2021). The democratisation myth: Open access and the solidification of epistemic injustices. *Science & Technology Studies, 34*(2), Article 2. 10.23987/sts.94964
Kreps, D. (Ed.). (2016). *Gramsci and Foucault: A reassessment.* Routledge.
Lee, C. J., Sugimoto, C. R., Zhang, G., & Cronin, B. (2013). Bias in peer review. *Journal of the American Society for Information Science and Technology, 64*(1), 2–17. 10.1002/asi.22784
Marx, K. (1887). *Capital: A critique of political economy (1st English edition).* Progress Publishers.

McGrath, A. E. (2019). *The territories of human reason: Science and theology in an age of multiple rationalities.* Oxford University Press.

Nanda, M. (2001). We are all hybrids now: The dangerous epistemology of post-colonial populism. *The Journal of Peasant Studies, 28*(2), 162–186. 10. 1080/03066150108438770

Nhemachena, A., Hlabangane, N., & Matowanyika, J. Z. Z. (Eds.). (2020). *Decolonising science, technology, engineering and mathematics (STEM) in an age of technocolonialism: Recentring African indigenous knowledge and belief systems.* Langaa RPCIG. 10.2307/j.ctv10h9fqz

Noda, O. (2020). Epistemic hegemony: The western straitjacket and post-colonial scars in academic publishing. *Revista Brasileira de Política Internacional, 63*(1). 10.1590/0034-7329202000107

Onie, S. (2020). Redesign open science for Asia, Africa and Latin America. *Nature, 587*(7832), 35–37. 10.1038/d41586-020-03052-3

Pearce, F., & Woodiwiss, T. (2001). Reading Foucault as a realist. In J. Lopez & G. Potter (Eds.), *After postmodernism: An introduction to critical realism* (pp. 51–62). Athlone Press.

Piron, F. (2018). Postcolonial open access. In U. Herb & J. Schopfel (Eds.), *Open divide: Critical studies in open access.* Litwin Books. http://hdl.handle.net/20. 500.11794/16178

Posholi, L. (2020). Epistemic decolonization as overcoming the hermeneutical injustice of Eurocentrism. *Philosophical Papers, 49*(2), 279–304. 10.1080/055 68641.2020.1779604

Prakash, G. (1994). Subaltern studies as postcolonial criticism. *The American Historical Review, 99*(5), 1475–1490. 10.2307/2168385

Rattansi, A. (1997). Postcolonialism and its discontents. *Economy and Society, 26*(4), 480–500. 10.1080/03085149700000025

Said, E. W. (1979). *Orientalism.* Vintage.

Santos, B. de S. (2016). *Epistemologies of the South: Justice against epistemicide.* Routledge.

Santos, B. de S. (2018). *The end of the cognitive empire: The coming of age of epistemologies of the South.* Duke University Press.

Sayer, A. (2012). Power, causality and normativity: A critical realist critique of Foucault. *Journal of Political Power, 5*(2), 179–194. 10.1080/2158379X.2012. 698898

Smith, C. (2010). *What is a person? Rethinking humanity, social life, and the moral good from the person up.* University of Chicago Press.

Spivak, G. C. (1988). Can the subaltern speak? In C. Nelson & L. Grossberg (Eds.), *Marxism and the interpretation of culture.* University of Illinois Press Urbana.

Stoddart, M. C. J. (2007). Ideology, hegemony, discourse: A critical review of theories of knowledge and power. *Social Thought & Research, 28,* 191–225.

Taylor, C. (1984). Foucault on freedom and truth. *Political Theory, 12*(2), 152–183.

Traynor, C., Foster, L., & Schonwetter, T. (2019). Tensions related to openness in researching indigenous peoples' knowledge systems and intellectual property rights. In L. Chan, A. Ratanawaraha, C. Neylon, H. Vessuri, & H. Thorsteinsdottir (Eds.), *Contextualizing openness: Situating open science* (pp. 223–236). University of Ottowa Press. https://ruor.uottawa.ca/handle/ 10393/39849

Volf, M. (2019). *Exclusion and embrace: A theological exploration of identity, otherness, and reconciliation (Revised and updated).* Abingdon Press.

Yegros-Yegros, A., van de Klippe, W., Abad-Garcia, M. F., & Rafols, I. (2020). Exploring why global health needs are unmet by research efforts: The potential influences of geography, industry and publication incentives. *Health Research Policy and Systems, 18*(1), 47. 10.1186/s12961-020-00560-6

Young, R. (1995). Foucault on race and colonialism. *New Formations, 25*, 57–65.

6 Epistemic openness and the "ecologies of knowledges"

Some recent work has taken postcolonial theory and its connection with knowledge in new directions that I want to discuss in this chapter. I will focus on the idea of the "ecologies of knowledges" championed by Boaventura de Sousa Santos which seems to offer a possible solution to the issues of relativism and incommensurability in a context of different epistemic systems, and therefore may help us to develop a rationale for OA and epistemic openness in a constructionist paradigm. His work has been used to frame critiques of many models of OA emanating from HICs, like APCs, and as a possible basis for reformative intervention (Albornoz et al., 2020). I will focus on two of his most influential books, *Epistemologies of the South* (2016) and *The End of the Cognitive Empire* (2018). I am going to argue that the "ecologies of knowledges" idea offers important insights, but despite that, it still leaves us with unresolved relativist and incommensurability dilemmas. That in turn means we still do not have a clear basis for establishing the validity or value of scientific knowledge, or a compelling rationale for sharing it.

Epistemologies of the South

In his influential book, *Epistemologies of the South*, Santos (2016) recognises many of the problems we have discussed and advocates an ethics-driven "interventionist" approach to knowledge conflicts. In his analysis, he presents an epistemology which relativises Western scientific knowledge, apparently locating his ideas within a thoroughgoing constructionist tradition:

> *The epistemic diversity of the world is open, since all knowledges are situated. The claim of the universal character of modern science is increasingly displayed as just one form of particularism, whose specificity consists of having the power to define all the knowledges that are its rivals as particularistic, local, contextual, and situational.*
> (Santos, 2016, p. 201)

DOI: 10.4324/9781032679259-6

By "science" Santos seems to mean STEMM disciplines plus at least some social sciences. In fact, most of his examples of the "cognitive injustice" of "science" come from the social sciences, and in particular, economics.

Santos argues that between this kind of scientific knowledge and other knowledges, including "epistemologies of the South", there is an epistemic "abyss". On one side of the abyss, scientific knowledge of the Global North is traditionally seen as objective, rational and reliable. On the other side of the abyss, other kinds of knowledges are perceived as "beliefs, opinions, intuitions, and subjective understandings". That includes non-Western knowledges, all of which are often considered invalid or irrelevant. Such "abyssal thinking", Santos argues, "consists in granting to modern science the monopoly of the universal distinction between true and false" (Santos, 2016, p. 119). Santos places Western philosophy and theology on the same side of the abyss as science, although with a lesser status. He also places Western law on that same side. Between them, these knowledges and associated practices represent a form of hegemony, a neo-colonial epistemic domination. He argues that "the struggle for global social justice must therefore be a struggle for global cognitive justice as well. In order to succeed, this struggle requires a new kind of thinking, a postabyssal thinking" (Santos, 2016, p. 124).

Seeing scientific knowledge as a vehicle for cognitive injustice, Santos argues that scientific openness cannot address the most important challenges in isolation: "There is no global social justice without global cognitive justice. The struggle for cognitive justice will not be successful if it depends exclusively on a more equitable distribution of scientific knowledge" (Santos, 2016, p. 207). Open access is not enough then, since the "more equitable distribution of scientific knowledge" is exactly what it is about. Rather, Santos proposes replacing "the hegemony of conventional epistemology and the consequent monoculture of scientific knowledge" (p. 207), with a recognition of "ecologies of knowledges", embracing both knowledges of the Global North and South.

The "ecologies of knowledges" is a very useful concept. The use of the metaphor of ecologies conveys the idea of a complex set of interactions and mutual reliances between knowledges enabling diverse growth. Santos argues that the epistemologies of the North should not be given the casting vote on knowledge claims but rather should be part of an ecology – a contention I am echoing in my argument for epistemic openness. Santos emphasises the importance of diversity of perspectives without any one perspective automatically being considered normative. He points out the potential for mutual enrichment across epistemic traditions. However, the interactions between knowledges may not be as natural or organic as the "ecology" metaphor implies. I believe it takes determined effort, sensitivity, and reflexivity to enable such interactions, as I have already suggested (Chapter 4). Nevertheless, the "ecology" metaphor does usefully help us understand an environment made up of complex relationships and dependencies between different parts that make up a larger system.

Nevertheless, I contend there are problems with Santos's analysis, two of which are particularly relevant to our discussion: first, his account of abyssal thinking; second, his views on relativism. On the first, I want to argue that Santos underplays the epistemic differences within what he calls "epistemologies of the North" whilst at the same time, overplaying the separation between those and "epistemologies of the South". As we have already seen, conventional scientific knowledge itself (understood broadly) already includes a range of quite different epistemic approaches – it is not the "monoculture" that Santos makes out. Agrawal (1995) made this point in discussing scientific knowledge, asking "by what yardstick of common measure, without creating completely meaningless categories, can one put together a Hume and a Foucault, a Derrida and a Von Neumann, or a Said and a Fogel?" (p. 13). Agrawal makes a similar point about differences between different indigenous knowledges. At the same time, Agrawal argues that sometimes elements of Western scientific thought might have more in common with corresponding areas of some indigenous knowledges than they do with other Western thought. It is in some of these areas, like environmental management, that we have already seen a willingness on the part of many involved to attempt to engage in an interaction between conventional scientific knowledge and non-Western knowledges. Of course, where those connections occur, Santos might say they are examples of "postabyssal thinking" – but at what point do we say that evidence of similarities and interactions between conventional science and other knowledge systems undermine the idea of an abyss in the first place?

Interestingly, in his own approach to knowledge, Santos attempts to distance himself from "Western, Eurocentric critical theory", and so therefore his work contains few direct references to thinkers such as Foucault and only limited references to Gramsci, for example. However, there are family resemblances between theirs and Santos's own analysis. Santos makes Gramscian-like use of the concept of hegemony. His discussion of "intercultural translation" is explicitly Gramscian (Santos, 2016, p. 212 ff). He also apparently bases his arguments on a Foucauldian-like relationship between knowledge and power (although the Foucauldian language of "discourses" is absent). Santos's notion of "struggles against domination" associated with "epistemologies of the South" (Santos, 2016, 2018, p. 65) also bears more than a passing resemblance to Foucault's idea of the "insurrection of subjugated knowledges" (Allen, 2017, p. 192; Foucault, 1980, p. 81). However, Santos does not share Foucault's reluctance to be drawn into making explicit value judgements, but rather renders explicit ethical judgements which remain implicit in poststructuralist analysis. He takes an ethically-driven interventionist position directed against "capitalism, colonialism and patriarchy" (Santos, 2016, p. 199), an approach that has a great deal in common with Gramsci and other neo-Marxist theorists. Santos's own analytical approach is based, even if implicitly, on Western tradition which is then brought into conversation with other knowledges.

On the second problem of Santos's thought, relativism, it is notable he recognises that his use of a constructionist paradigm might be challenged in terms of the incommensurability problem, and is keen to assert that "the ecologies of knowledges does not entail accepting relativism" (Santos, 2016, p. 190). He explains this by setting out a different kind of meta-theory required by his interventionist position: "the ecologies of knowledge is constructivist as concerns representation and realist as concerns intervention" (p. 207). He describes this as "pragmatic realism" (Santos, 2016, p. 207), but he provides little explanation of what he actually means, although he does relate it in passing to the philosophical school of pragmatism. He uses "pragmatic realism" as a basis for arguing for an "equality of opportunity" when considering the relative merits of ideas from different knowledges, based, he says, on their "respective contributions towards building 'another possible world'" (p. 190), that is, achieving positive real-world change.

Santos does, however, recognise the possibility of a "choice among alternative interventions in the same social domain in which different knowledges collide" (Santos, 2016, p. 205). In these cases, he argues, it is important to achieve "judgments not based on abstract hierarchies between knowledges but stemming from democratic deliberations about gains and losses" (p. 205). In other words, he is advocating an outcomes-based approach, side-stepping epistemic validity, and based on an assessment of probable outcomes. He returns to this line of thinking in *Epistemic Empires* (discussed below). In *Epistemologies of the South*, however, he talks about these dilemmas in terms of "intercultural translation" – a kind of conversation of knowledges. Whilst he spends some time usefully explaining how this conversation can take place in later chapters of the *Epistemologies of the South*, he does not explain how questions of relativism and incommensurability might be resolved by it.

Epistemic empires

In a more recent work, *The End of the Cognitive Empire* (2018), Santos explores in further detail how scientific knowledge of the Global North is a vehicle for domination over the South and he develops some of the ideas he proposed in his earlier work. Santos argues again that it is essential to recognise the importance of "the diversity of the experiences of the world, together with a conversation of the world that takes them seriously" (p. 38). He argues that this conversation cannot happen if one perspective, a Northern perspective, is "forcefully imposed" on all others (Santos, 2018, p. 38). He identifies a large number of questions arising from his project, which the book goes on to address. The very first question he addresses is that of relativism, a challenge to which he is obviously sensitive. It is interesting that, despite his attempts to distance himself from Western theory, at this crucial point, Santos sides with Foucault:

> *Foucault clearly shows in* The Archaeology of Knowledge *that the philosophy of science, or epistemology in the conventional sense, is not external to the science the validity of whose foundations it investigates. Both are based on the same cultural presuppositions, or epistemes, to use Foucault's own term.*
>
> (Santos, 2018, p. 37)

The implications of this are significant for approaching the relativism and incommensurability problem – but not in achieving a resolution. If justification for claims made within a particular knowledge system can only be developed within that same system, then no common criteria can be applied to competing claims derived from different knowledge systems, even if the different claims are apparently incompatible. This seems to be an admission that the problem of relativism and incommensurability are irresolvable within Santos's analysis.

Santos, however, proposes a different set of criteria for the validity of knowledges in the context of his project: "knowledges are to be evaluated and ultimately validated according to their usefulness in maximizing the possibilities of success of the struggles against oppression." (Santos, 2018, p. 38). This is apparently the "pragmatic realism" that Santos mentioned in his earlier work. It seems to be an ethical test to establish the validity of knowledge. Santos states that different knowledge claims should be determined by the extent to which they enhance "resistance against capitalism, colonialism, and patriarchy". It is ironic that Santos criticises "antirelativists" as being guilty of running a "moral crusade" in their approach to knowledge. His own perspective is clearly a moralist, activist one.

At this point, it becomes difficult to see how Santos is doing anything but replacing one universal set of criteria to assess the validity of knowledge with another. Instead of criteria normally applied to judge the validity of knowledge (empirical evidence, coherence, simplicity, etc), he replaces those with a different single set of criteria – which relate to the extent to which knowledge can help to address injustice. This raises the problem of how are we to judge the extent knowledge does this? Who is to say? If we are to assess the validity of knowledge in terms of its utility in combating injustice, how are we to judge what constitutes injustice in the first place? Santos is clearly using criteria to make such judgements himself in his condemnation of what he regards as oppressive, but the criteria he uses are not made transparent. Instead, he seems to regard the ways we identify injustice as self-evident. However, we need clarity on this to determine how disputes about injustices (on what constitutes an injustice) can be resolved. For example, if different communities see each other's actions as being oppressive to each other, how can such disputed claims be resolved? And by whom? It is difficult to see how Santos's view that the epistemic community of the oppressed should decide could resolve this kind of disputed situation.

In any case, Santos's view of how knowledge is validated seems remarkably narrow. How can such criteria be applied to all knowledge claims? It is possible that Santos's position about assessing the validity of knowledge is only meant to apply to a restricted set of claims, those that specifically relate to emancipatory questions, for example. If this is the case, his position is designed to be a pragmatic way to inform action associated with social interventions – although, if it is, it still runs into the problem just discussed of how to resolve disputed claims of injustice. It also does not provide any grounds for addressing general problems of incommensurability.

Alternatively, Santos's position may work at a kind of meta level, applied to systems of thought, rather than individual knowledge claims. Santos emphasises that different knowledge systems have their own internal means of evaluation, and so he recognises the value of Western science when harnessed for the liberatory purposes he espouses. In this case, it is possible to see the validity test he proposes as a kind of meta-test of knowledges. Every knowledge claim can be assessed within its own knowledge system, but across knowledge systems his ethical criteria then apply to a knowledge system's overall validity in furthering emancipation. Such a view looks somewhat more credible than applying the ethical evaluation criteria to all knowledge claims, although it is not clear this *is* what Santos means.

Even if this is what he means, Santos's view still retains the problems of relativism and incommensurability. The question remains, how can such competing knowledge claims of what constitutes injustice be assessed relative to each other? And in relation to the question of the validity of knowledge claims in general, how can competing claims from different knowledge systems be assessed in relation to each other? Taking the Foucauldian line, the claims favoured by the most powerful would gain the upper hand since power and knowledge are so closely intertwined. But it is precisely that (that dominant knowledge claims reflect the will of the most powerful) that Santos is arguing should not happen.

The argument I am making is that if epistemic openness is to fulfil its full potential, it should mean dialogue between different epistemic systems and not just their disconnected coexistence. Santos's idea of "intercultural translation" seems to imply this but I would suggest that dialogue between knowledges means considering different ideas together, exploring their possible relationships, and, crucially, testing their relative merits against each other. Santos's project associated with the "ecologies of knowledges" seems at first to offer the possibility of doing this, but, I suggest, does not fully deliver on that promise. There is no epistemic basis for addressing the problem of how the validity of different ideas from different epistemic systems can be tested in relation to each other. Santos seems at first sight to attempt to retrieve what appears to be a position relying on a thoroughgoing constructionist paradigm, and social theory on which it is based, from the relativist dilemma, but, like much social theory based on an apparently thorough-going constructionism, the role of ontology is only cursorily addressed, except to claim a "pragmatic realism". Santos's own definition that his project is "constructivist as concerns representation and realist as concerns intervention" aims to combine constructionism and realism, but the way in which he does so seems to create a tension that is difficult to hold together. Moreover, his approach seems to be based on shaky foundations in relation to ethical judgements, which themselves are not grounded (Taylor, 1984). How an ethically-driven interventionist approach can be reconciled with this relativist paradigm remains unresolved.

Whilst we can learn a great deal from the "ecologies of knowledges" project, it still leaves us with the major challenge of how relativism and incommensurability might be addressed. Thinking through how this problem can begin to be addressed is likely to help to retrieve the case for scientific and epistemic openness from the cul-de-sac into which social theory based on thoroughgoing constructionism has led them. It also helps to push back against the argument that wants to position OA primarily as an oppressive force, and which pictures the knowledge disseminated via OA channels as a discourse that is simply a function of power. We will begin to explore possible approaches to addressing these challenges in the next chapter.

References

Agrawal, A. (1995). Dismantling the divide between indigenous and scientific knowledge. *Development and Change, 26*(3), 413–439. 10.1111/j.1467-7660. 1995.tb00560.x. Preprint: https://hdl.handle.net/10535/4201

Albornoz, D., Okune, A., & Chan, L. (2020). Can open scholarly practices redress epistemic injustice? In M. P. Eve & J. Gray (Eds.), *Reassembling scholarly communications: Histories, infrastructures, and global politics of open access.* 10.7551/mitpress/11885.003.0009

Allen, A. (2017). Power/knowledge/resistance: Foucault and epistemic injustice. In I. J. Kidd, J. Medina, & G. Pohlhaus (Eds.), *The Routledge handbook of epistemic injustice* (pp. 187–194). Routledge.

Foucault, M. (1980). *Power/knowledge: Selected interviews and other writings, 1972-1977 (C. Gordon, Trans.; 1st American ed.)*. Pantheon Books.

Santos, B. de S. (2016). *Epistemologies of the South: Justice against epistemicide.* Routledge.

Santos, B. de S. (2018). *The end of the cognitive empire: The coming of age of epistemologies of the South.* Duke University Press.

Taylor, C. (1984). Foucault on freedom and truth. *Political Theory, 12*(2), 152–183.

7 Epistemic openness and critical realism

In this chapter, I want to outline a meta-theoretical position that accommodates a range of knowledge forms, allowing epistemic openness, but at the same time, does not involve relinquishing the idea that different propositions may have greater demonstrable validity than others. I will argue that this position, summarised under the label 'critical realism', has significant explanatory power as a meta-theoretical undergirding for research. It helps us to navigate between the extremes of (adapted-) positivism and thoroughgoing constructionism, and it can also assist in recognising the value of openness. I will argue that critical realism helps us to understand how epistemic openness can work – its character and its limits. I will also argue that critical realism provides a useful basis for making the case for open access. I will go on to discuss social theory compatible with critical realism and its relationship with the case for openness, which I will argue is a strong one. I will illustrate my discussion with engagement with meta-theory and social theory developed by critical realists such as Roy Bhaskar, Margaret Archer, Christian Smith, and Dave Elder-Vass. I will also discuss social theory compatible with critical realism, such as commons theory, which has been explicitly used to frame open access by its founder Elinor Ostrom and others. I will suggest that an approach based on critical realism can help us navigate many of the debates around OA where advocates of OA and its critics are often talking past each other without finding the language or concepts to engage with each other's arguments.

Critical realism

Critical realism is a realist position that at the same time accommodates "moderate" or "weak" constructionism but rejects "radical" or "strong" constructionism (Elder-Vass, 2012). Elder-Vass summarises this position:

> *Realists divide the world into that which depends on how we (individually or collectively) think about it and that which does not. For realists – and*

DOI: 10.4324/9781032679259-7

moderate constructionists – only the former can be socially constructed; the latter cannot. Radical constructionists tend to deny any such distinction on the grounds that everything *depends on the ways in which we think about it, or at least to include in the socially constructed category things that realists would not.*

(Elder-Vass, 2012, p. 6, emphasis original)

As an example of combining realism and constructionism, Elder-Vass cites Bourdieu's (1979) exploration of class, which is based on a detailed analysis of the material – wealth, income, geography and so on – with the socially constructed – culture, dispositions, taste and so on. Hints of this have emerged in my discussion earlier in relation to the knowledge-as-oppression argument, the 'softer' version of which identifies the importance of biases involving a range of material and socially constructed issues interacting with each other – such as empirical data gathered entirely from Western participants used as the basis for generating explanatory theory then assumed to be universally applicable.

Elder-Vass (2012) uses the terminology of "moderate" and "radical" constructionism; Sayer (2000) and Smith (2010) distinguish between "weak" and "strong" constructionism, to make the same point. Smith defines "weak" constructionism in the following way:

All human knowledge is conceptually mediated and can be and usually is influenced by particular and contingent sociocultural factors such as material interests, group structures, linguistic categories, technological development, and the like – such that what people believe to be real is significantly shaped not only by objective reality but also by their sociocultural contexts. Furthermore, there is a dimension of reality that humans socially construct, what I will refer to … as institutional facts, that is, those aspects of the real that humans think, speak, and interact into existence.

(Smith, 2010, p. 122)

Crucially, this is distinguished from "strong" or "radical" construc-tionism because of its emphasis on knowledge being only "mediated … and influenced by" contingent factors (see Smith's definition of "strong constructionism" quoted in Chapter 5), although some social systems, or "institutional facts", are socially constructed. That is different from "strong" or thoroughgoing or radical constructionist claims, such as Burr's claim that "what we know as reality is itself a construction" (Burr, 2015, p. 92) or Foucault's 'bracketing off' of questions of reality because of its inaccessibility apart from discourses.

Critical realism is a realist constructionist paradigm that I want to argue has considerable explanatory power and I suggest provides a useful frame for understanding how epistemic openness can work. It means that we can value different contributions to knowledge, and, at the same time, gives us grounds for subjecting knowledge to critical scrutiny. I will also argue it provides undergirding for social theory which itself enlarges our understanding of OA, and which can frame action aiming to achieve a more equitable scholarly communication system. In addition, I want to observe that epistemic openness and scientific openness, the latter particularly in the form of open access, are mutually reinforcing. I will suggest epistemic openness understood within a critical realist frame, provides strong grounds for promoting open access to encourage wide dissemination of different contributions to knowledge. At the same time, OA enables epistemic openness, by disseminating different kinds of knowledge widely, promoting beneficial exchanges between and within knowledges.

Critical realism is designed to avoid the problems of both (adapted-) positivism and radical constructionism, and in doing so aims to provide more explanatory power in relation to the world and our experience of it (Sayer, 2000). We have seen that (adapted-) positivism favours a realist ontology and objectivist epistemology, holding that the real world 'out there' can be known and understood through scientific investigation, and that the knowledge produced can be universal and objective. However, in doing so it fails to take account of the constructedness and the situatedness of knowledge. In contrast, radical constructionism, based on subjectivist and relativist views of knowledge, would hold that Western science is no more valid than other kinds of epistemologies and is actually the product of social forces, particularly systems of power. However, in calling out positivism's (overly-) confident objectivist epistemology, thoroughgoing constructionism can be criticised as failing to advance a credible view of reality consistent with our own experiences, particularly in failing to recognise the existence of aspects of reality that are "intransitive", existent outside of human experience (Elder-Vass, 2012). A radical constructionist view of the world, for example, fails to satisfactorily account for the demonstrable success of science and technology in understanding and manipulating the real world.

Anti-positivist constructionist meta-theory was developed partly to address ways in which positivism conflates ontology and epistemology, but arguably radical constructionism also conflates the two, albeit in a different way. Positivist and adapted-positivist meta-theory conflate ontology and epistemology by confusing objective reality with our knowledge of it, as though they are one and the same thing – our understanding of reality is unmediated and direct. This gives primacy to ontology and devalues epistemology. On the other hand, radical constructionism, by seeing knowledge as constructing reality, disallows the existence of any objective reality (or, at least, any meaningful knowledge of it). This gives primacy to epistemology and devalues ontology. Thus, in the relation between the object and the knower, (adapted-) positivist theory places too much emphasis on the object and not enough on the knower (and their situatedness); thoroughgoing constructionist theory places too much emphasis on the knower and not enough on the object (in its own right) (Wright, 2014). Both tend towards insisting on epistemic foreclosure: positivism by saying that certain facts once uncovered are known, and that is that; radical constructionism, by saying that all epistemologies are equally valid and therefore the relative merits of competing claims made within different epistemic systems cannot be meaningfully tested in relation to each other. Both positions are clearly problematic.

There are a group of realist meta-theories that attempt to avoid the difficulties associated with both modernist (adapted-) positivist and postmodernist anti-positivist meta-theory (Maxwell & Mittapalli, 2010) and which, I want to argue, give us strong explanatory power. These different forms of realism have been given different labels ('critical realism', 'scientific realism', as well as others) but they have similar fundamental features. I am calling these related theories, 'critical realism', but it is important to recognise that, like positivism and anti-positivism, critical realism is not a single, easily definable belief, but rather a set of positions, more or less common to those who represent this approach, but defined and explained in varying ways (Elder-Vass, 2021; Sayer, 2000).

There are other meta-theoretical frameworks that inhabit the space between (adapted-) positivist and anti-positivist constructionist meta-theory, one of which is pragmatism (Bernstein, 1992). Miedema (2022) uses pragmatism, rather than critical realism, as a basis for contending for the importance of open science. Although some pragmatists and critical realists have sought to make hard distinctions between their positions, others point out that they share a great deal, at the same time acknowledging that both are quite broad churches (Elder-Vass, 2022). I agree with much of Meidema's argument for supporting open science in that it enables the "sharing of ideas and experimental results and methods, for debate and scrutiny in a rigorous and communitive process by the community of inquirers" (Miedema, 2022, p. 62). The practical outcomes for which I am arguing here are compatible with those of Miedema in many respects, although I am suggesting that a critical realist position provides a particularly satisfying framing for the case for openness in science for reasons that I will go on to discuss.

One prominent theorist of critical realism is Roy Bhaskar (1979, 1989), often regarded as its founder. His meta-theory was initially developed to inform a philosophy of science but was later extended to social theory. It consists of three main pillars: (1) realist ontology,

(2) relativist epistemology, and (3) judgmental rationality. There is (1) a real world out there, separate from our experience of it. However, (2) our knowledge of reality is always subjective, contingent, and therefore contestable. As Bhaskar puts it:

> *If the objects of our knowledge exist and act independently of the knowledge of which they are the objects, it is equally the case that such knowledge as we may actually possess always consists in historically specific social forms.*
>
> (Bhaskar, 2015, p. 11)

However, that does not mean 'anything goes'. Rather, (3) we can discern different levels of validity between different propositions. It is possible to make reasonable, justified judgements about reality, for example, giving weight to those epistemological positions with the best demonstrable purchase on ontological reality. As summarised by Elder-Vass (2021), the three pillars of critical realism mean:

> *If one accepts that there is a real world that is largely external to and independent of any one observer and her beliefs about it, and that we have some capacity to be influenced in our beliefs by that world, then it follows that our beliefs can be proven wrong by further experience.*
>
> (Elder-Vass, 2021, p. 243)

There are grounds then for exploring the real world through empirical analyses and theory development in order to provide insight that can be tested and refined or replaced on an ongoing basis.

The epistemic foreclosure that is characteristic of positivism and radical constructionist anti-positivism is not a problem with critical realism. Whilst it does hold a relativist epistemology, compatible with its moderate constructionism, it balances constructionism with judgemental rationality, such that there can be meaningful debate and discussion on how best to characterise reality. A variety of epistemologies can coexist at different explanatory levels in what Bhaskar (2010) calls a "laminated totality", but are all subject to comparative testing based in large part on the extent to which they usefully explain our experience of the world. One theory can trump another if it has greater explanatory power. Wright (2014) in the context of philosophy and theology identifies these criteria for judging between theories or other ideas in a critical realist context: "congruence with life experience, internal coherence, fertility, simplicity, and illuminatory depth". Smith (2010) associates our ability to make such judgements with key human "capacities" – "well-fitted perception, experience of practical adequacy, and rational evaluation of coherence" (p. 215) – which can form the basis of choosing between truth claims. It is important to emphasise that this does not imply a single, fixed judgemental rationality, but is likely to involve multiple rationalities (McGrath, 2019). Unlike most radical constructionist approaches, critical realism, similar to positivism, focuses on causation, but, unlike positivism, defines this in terms of "tendencies" rather than "exceptionless regularities", taking into account complex open systems that are present in the real world (Elder-Vass, 2021; Smith, 2010).

Bhaskar's proposal that we understand reality as a "laminated totality" is worth exploring further, particularly, as I will argue, it fits well with encouraging greater openness in scholarly communication. Bhaskar (2015) argues that reality is "stratified and differentiated" (p. 6) and that this determines the way that a given phenomenon is investigated – there may be physical, biological, or social objects of investigation that need to be investigated differently. Moreover, different layers of explanation deriving from different epistemic systems can usefully contribute to a holistic understanding of a single phenomenon. Methodological and theoretical pluralism are important aspects of this. McGrath (2019) uses the idea of "disability" to explain such pluralism. "Disability" may be discussed, according to the World Health Organisation (WHO) in terms of "pathology" (such as abnormality of a particular human organ), "impairment" (such as that resulting in changes in the whole human body), "activity" (such as restrictions arising from the interaction between a person and their environment) or "participation" (such as involvement in social situations). This means that disability can be explained in terms of a whole range of epistemic traditions, from biology to sociology, using different methods and based on different theoretical assumptions, all of which contribute to a "laminated totality".

A critical realist paradigm allows for an understanding of reality that is multifaceted, with those facets acting upon each other, and one which requires ongoing discussion and testing, something I suggest is compatible with greater openness. Exposing different claims to scrutiny is part of a fruitful academic conversation. In his critical realist account of personhood, Smith discusses the need to find "best accounts" of reality and our experience, interacting with the ideas of Charles Taylor, describing how this can be approached:

> *Best accounts are arrived at by challenge, discussion, argumentation, reflection, criticism, vetting, that is, by testing against the clarity of experience, including through systematic observation and the discipline of reason.*
>
> (Smith, 2010, p. 112)

Open access, I want to argue, can make such academic conversations easier, since it makes available a wide range of literatures, such that different sorts of knowledge can all be brought to bear on a particular issue. The BOAI (2002) uses the term "conversation" in this sense. A critical realist perspective on the argument for scientific and epistemic openness would then ostensibly engender a positive view of scholarly communication in general, and OA in particular, in that it enables the wide circulation of different knowledge claims. Combined with epistemic openness, OA facilitates a multi-layered set of perspectives on reality comprising different rationalities, disciplinary approaches, theories, and methods, all of which may have something to contribute to our understanding of the world. I am arguing that this multi-layered set of perspectives should include contributions generated within a Western academic context alongside others generated within different epistemic traditions. Sharing in this way is likely to help to counter exclusionary scientistic assumptions or Northern-centricity in scholarship.

However, it is important to note, this does not amount to an argument for the epistemic parity of all knowledge claims or of epistemic validity determined by positionality. Of course, perspectives based on positionality, such as an individual's lived experience, are likely to lead to significant insights and to be immensely valuable (and I want to discuss the value of multiple perspectives further in arguing for participatory openness, in Chapter 8). Bringing different perspectives into conversation with each other can often cast new light on a problem, and there is a pressing need for epistemic and cultural humility to make that conversation work. However, positionality is not an epistemic trump card. Over-reliance on positionality alone can very quickly lead to a proliferation of irreconcilable perspectives without any hope of resolution: the problems of relativism and incommensurability. All different perspectives need to be tested using the judgemental rationalities available to us, in which a crucial factor is the tests listed by Wright (2014) above ("congruence with life experience, internal coherence", etc.) using the capacities identified by Smith (2010) above ("well-fitted perception", "experience of practical adequacy", etc). There needs to be a dialogue between different perspectives in which the scholarly literature and other knowledge inputs can play their part. I contend that OA accompanied by epistemic openness can help establish a pluriform knowledge pool, and also an environment in which ideas are tested, and thus enable a meaningful ongoing conversation.

Critical realism, social theory, and OA

As part of Bhaskar's investigation of social science theories, he developed an approach to account for change in society based on critical realism, the Transformational Model of Social Action (TMSA) (Bhaskar, 1979, 1989). TMSA was developed based on the acknowledgement that social systems are different from natural systems. Social systems are, for example, always "open" systems, characterised by complexity which cannot be artificially "closed" for purposes of analysis. Many STEMM approaches, in contrast, create artificially closed systems, in carrying out experiments, with limited numbers of possible variables. Social analysis cannot normally do that. Social analysis often focuses on the "transitive" (that is constructed perspectives on reality) as well as "intransitive" objects, which are the focus of much of natural science. As well as analytical utility, Bhaskar also wanted his social theory to have an emancipatory value, enabling not merely a better understanding of social phenomena but also beneficial change.

Like much social theory, Bhaskar's focused on the relationship between structure and agency, between social systems and human actions. He recognised that social change occurred as a result of an interplay between the two. Bhaskar's theories have been taken up and developed by other social theorists, notably Margaret Archer (1995, 2000). Archer's theory of morphogenesis, developed and refined in the 1980s and 90s, was explicitly based on critical realism and involved an explanation of how structure and agency relate to each other over time. Archer draws attention to the fact that some social analysis places undue emphasis on structure, under-estimating the importance of agency, what she calls "downwards conflation" (Archer, 1995). The opposite is also possible: undue emphasis being placed on the importance of agency, underplaying the importance of structure, "upwards conflation". Crudely speaking, Marxist and neo-Marxist explanations emphasise the importance of social systems and therefore tend towards "downwards conflation". Liberal perspectives, on the other hand, rely on individualism as a form of explanation and, therefore, tend towards "upwards conflation". In contrast, Archer's theory gives prominence to both structure and agency, and how they interact. In doing so, however, she maintains a careful distinction between the two. She distinguishes between structure and agency in terms of time, showing how pre-existing structures can be transformed by human action resulting either in reproduction ("morphostasis") or transformation ("morphogenesis") of structures. She states, "(i) that structure necessarily pre-dates the action(s) which transform it ... and; (ii) ... that structural elaboration necessarily post-dates those actions which have transformed it" (Archer, 1995, p. 157). Carrying out analysis with this understanding allows the different components of social change to be disentangled. This relationship applies to cultural as much as other social change, where cultural conditioning is subject to socio-cultural interaction leading to cultural change or stasis. Agents are not necessarily conceived of in highly atomised individualised ways but also relationally, as parts of groups and communities – sometimes defined as 'personalism', as opposed to 'individualism' (Smith, 2010).

This kind of social theory based explicitly on the meta-theoretical foundations of critical realism provides a useful basis on which to develop an understanding of the OA debate we are investigating. It has, I believe, greater explanatory power than at least some aspects of either a critical approach, which tends towards downwards conflation, or liberalism, which tends towards upwards conflation. The theory helps us to see a scholarly communication environment with complex social and cultural structures, developed over many years, providing the conditioning for any developments. Social and cultural interactions occur in a large range of ways, which are then elaborated in the structures and cultures of the research community. As far as change is concerned, perhaps some of the most significant agential actions relate to policy development – where the contributions of relatively small numbers of policy officers and their advisors can have significant morphogenic outcomes. We see this happening in the history of OA, where well-formed policy can have significant effects on the system as a whole (Larivière & Sugimoto, 2018).

One theory illustrative of a number of the issues discussed in relation to meta-theory and which has been used in understanding OA is commons theory (Hess & Ostrom, 2007; Johnson, 2019). Commons theory is not explicitly built on critical realism, unlike Archer's morphogenesis. It is, however, compatible with critical realism, and, I would argue, incompatible with positivism or radical constructionism. Commons theory takes a basically realist perspective on social and economic systems (Lewis, 2021), shaped by their relationships with material circumstances, showing how communities can achieve collective management of common pool resources. This realism immediately puts it at odds with radical constructionism. Commons theory does, however, recognise the importance of social structures and of the way they construct social understandings of reality – a seemingly moderate constructionist position. Both physical conditions and social structures are seen as contributing to a particular "action area". With regard to social structures, commons theory shows how communities can achieve governance of shared resources through institutions, sets of rules and mechanisms for implementing them, which oversee the use of shared resources. There is a voluntary collective pooling of power amongst community members for mutual benefit. Power in this case is not an imposition but more of a cooperative network. It is also important to note that commons theory is not inherently anti-market or anti-statist (Sarker & Blomquist, 2019), but rather holds that in certain circumstances these are not the best solutions, particularly where communities themselves can agree on means of governing their own practices. Crucially, commons theory draws knowledge from different cultures and regions, including indigenous communities based in LMICs, in order to understand how commons approaches are constructed. In this way, a commons approach can draw on knowledge from a particular non-Western epistemic tradition to explain an action area, which is incorporated into a multi-layered understanding of reality to inform action. Hess and Ostrom (2007) give an example of how commons theory has been used to "analyze governance and Aboriginal participation in forest management in Canada" (p. 43) amongst a range of other uses.

The founder of commons theory, Elinor Ostrom, herself engaged with open access using her theory along with a collaborator, Charlotte Hess (Hess & Ostrom, 2007). They focused on the process of setting up a digital OA repository seen through the lens of the Institutional Analysis and Development framework, an analytical tool for understanding the factors involved in commons situations. Commons theory has been taken up by others to frame explanations of OA (Ballantyne, 2022) and open science (Frischmann et al., 2014), and as a way of talking about community-based publishing approaches in contrast to a highly-commercialised knowledge market (Bosman et al., 2017). This knowledge commons approach to publishing has self-governance of publishing by academic communities at its heart and enables publishing to become an integral feature of the research process by not outsourcing that role to commercial interests which do not necessarily share the same values and priorities of the research community.

Overcoming epistemic barriers in LMICs

The argument I am making for epistemic openness relates to issues of coloniality and neo-coloniality and their connection with contemporary knowledge and its relationship with oppressive power. It may be useful at this point to consider these issues through the lens of critical realism. The first pillar of critical realism is realist ontology. This involves the recognition of the importance of materiality in social development and relations, including those between global regions and their economies. Coloniality and neo-coloniality have had and continue to have major negative material consequences for people in LMICs, demonstrable regardless of the perspective of the observer, and knowledge claims need to take account of and be anchored on ontological reality. Second, is epistemological relativism. My argument builds on a recognition of the importance of the constructedness and situatedness of knowledge, and the existence of different knowledge systems with validity. Epistemological relativism means we need to search for best accounts, a challenge which creates an incentive where relevant to bring conventional academic knowledge into conversation with other knowledges. That conversation, I am arguing, does not necessarily involve sliding into irresolvable relativism, because of the importance of judgemental rationality, the third pillar of critical realism. The argument for epistemic openness is not that anything goes. Rather, the merits of different claims need to be tested, and some can then be recognised as having greater validity, even if uncertainty remains. This realist social constructionism does involve letting go of some aspects of power/knowledge theory and hegemony theory based on radical constructionism, but it frees us from the inevitable irresolvable relativism associated with radical constructionism. Realist social constructionism also gives us the basis for developing an ethics-based emancipatory agenda around open access, whilst still subjecting openness itself in its different forms to necessary critique.

From this meta-theoretical foundation, I have argued that it is important to recognise that major epistemic barriers exist to greater global knowledge equity, and that they are extremely difficult to overcome. Scientific knowledge generation can (and often does) involve major biases, many of which reflect and reinforce global inequities (discussed in Chapter 5). Addressing these barriers, however challenging, is crucial because doing so will help to strengthen the usefulness of knowledge generated by science in a range of different global contexts. As an illustration, in Chapter 4, we explored the value of interactions between conventional scientific knowledge and other knowledges, including indigenous knowledges. The argument I have been making is one which recognises the global importance of science, but at the same time acknowledges that to interact with other knowledges, science may often need to change in order to be genuinely global. Greater epistemic openness, I contend, is an essential part of that change. We have seen, albeit briefly, what such change might look like, in considering interactions between scientific and indigenous knowledges in Chapter 4, and in addressing biases in Chapter 5. In this way, epistemic openness becomes an important means of addressing hermeneutical epistemic injustice. At the same time, I have argued earlier in this chapter, there needs to be acceptance that all knowledges need to be subject to scrutiny.

The argument of Havemann et al. (2020) in the context of the COVID-19 pandemic seems to reflect the kind of balance for which I am arguing. It involves including indigenous knowledges in our understanding of health, but *at the same time* subjecting them to scrutiny alongside conventional medical science. Their approach combining scrutiny with respect in relation to indigenous medicine, in this case, is best mediated through African scientists, who understand the context and can engage in the interaction between conventional medical science and indigenous knowledges sensitively (Havemann et al., 2020). This kind of approach can help us address competing claims within and between different epistemic systems. Smith (2010) summarises this approach from a critical realist perspective:

> *How can we adjudicate among competing, plausible accounts of the same reality? The answer is that we must proceed with the only noncoercive option available. That is to continue to interrogate the adequacy of our ideas and explanations, to gather more evidence promising to shed new light, and to continue to hammer away at the best account of reality through collective discussion, argumentation, reflection, and criticism – in sum, again, testing our accounts against the clarity of experience through systematic observation and the discipline of reason.*
>
> (Smith, 2010, p. 218)

Openness, I am arguing, can help us to achieve that necessary continual evidence gathering, testing of ideas, and discussion needed, and this can happen across epistemic boundaries just as much as within them, albeit with careful and sensitive handling.

It is sometimes claimed that a thoroughgoing relativist view might encourage the same practical outcome, encouraging dialogue between and within different epistemic systems. However, my argument is that a relativist position does not give us grounds for such a practical response, or any kind of obligation to adopt such practices. In fact, like Groff (2004), I believe anti-positivist relativism actually pushes us in the opposite direction:

> *If all beliefs about the world are equally valid, then no claims may be challenged on cognitive, or epistemic, grounds. At best, relativism can therefore be expected to discourage critical analysis and exchange – for what is the point of attempts to persuade through argumentation, if all claims about the world are by definition equally valid? At worst, it implies that critical exchange ought to be abandoned in favor of the use of force and/or non-rational charismatic appeals.*
>
> (Groff, 2004, p. 1)

Rather than abandoning scholarly conversations, I am proposing that they ought to be extended to take in other knowledge forms, and that openness helps us to do so.

The fact of epistemological relativism means that judgemental rationality needs to be exercised in a way that involves an often-underrated quality in knowledge development: epistemic humility. Humility, emphasised by Oreskes (2019) as being essential for engendering trust in science, is, I suggest, most likely to result in robust knowledge formation since it represents a willingness to listen to and consider other perspectives. At the same time, judgemental rationality means that as well as recognising the value of different epistemic systems, including indigenous knowledge systems, we cannot dispense with criticality in relation to any system, including indigenous knowledges. Moosavi (2020) warns we should "guard against an exaggerate [sic] romanticisation or unwarranted flattery" of knowledge from the Global South (p. 347). There needs to be room for the critical assessment of all systems of knowledge, resisting assumed "epistemic parity" if it deflects criticality in relation to indigenous knowledges. An approach uncritical of indigenous knowledges, Nanda comments, "ends up immunizing the objectively false and socially regressive elements of indigenous knowledge systems of non-Western societies from critical evaluation and reform" (Nanda, 2001, pp. 183–184). The same should be said of claims made within Western knowledge systems, of course. Criticality needs to operate in all directions.

It is important to resist the "binarizing strategy" of at least some postcolonial analysis (Mannathukkaren, 2010), including some analyses of OA. 'Global North' versus 'Global South', 'modern' versus 'traditional', 'oppressor' versus 'oppressed', 'epistemologies of the North' versus 'epistemologies of the South', are all common examples of such binaries. Countries and regions are all too often characterised as epistemic monoliths and in a way that is predominantly oppositional: 'the West versus the rest'. There is a clear danger of reductionism in such an approach. Vickers, in his outspoken response to postcolonialism from the point of view of a comparative educationalist, comments, "the result is a target for the 'decolonial' argument that is large, diffuse, and readily distinguishable from a 'periphery' defined by shared experience of oppression or marginalisation" (Vickers, 2020, p. 170). We see this dichotomous thinking in much of the critique of OA, for example, with ideas of the 'core' and 'periphery' being applied to scholarly communication (Mboa Nkoudou, 2020; Piron, 2018). Providing explanations in terms of a binary, Mannathukkaren (2010) argues, misses the "'continuous dynamic causal interaction' between the different halves of the binary and the ways in which they are bridged" (Mannathukkaren, 2010, p. 318, quoting Bhaskar, 1989, p. 6). Even if certain binarising concepts still seem useful, they need to be used with care. Waisbich et al. (2021) make that point about the concept of the 'Global South' and the need to avoid telling "one single story" about the Global South, but rather to discern "'Global South' polyphonies" – multiple voices telling multiple stories.

To reiterate, the interactions and exchanges that I am arguing are characteristic of epistemic openness need to be handled sensitively and respectfully. It is essential to listen to multiple voices and multiple stories with epistemic humility. It is in that context that meaningful discussion and critique can best occur. Such meaningful interaction and genuine exchange can also best happen if participation in the conversation is as open as possible. It is to the question of participation that we turn in the next chapter.

References

Archer, M. S. (1995). *Realist social theory: The morphogenetic approach.* Cambridge University Press.

Archer, M. S. (2000). *Being human: The problem of agency.* Cambridge University Press.

Ballantyne, N. (2022). Scholarly publication, open access and the commons. *Critical and Radical Social Work*, 1–15. 10.1332/204986021X16467538565525

Bernstein, R. J. (1992). The resurgence of pragmatism. *Social Research, 59*(4), 813–840.

Bhaskar, R. (1979). *The possibility of naturalism.* Atlantic Highlands.

Bhaskar, R. (1989). *Reclaiming reality.* Verso.

Bhaskar, R. (2010). Contexts of interdisciplinarity: Interdisciplinarity and climate change. In R. Bhaskar, C. Frank, K. G. Høyer, P. Næss, & J. Parker (Eds.), *Interdisciplinarity and climate change: Transforming knowledge and practice for our global future.* Routledge. https://www.taylorfrancis.com/books/e/978113 6996702/chapters/10.4324%2F9780203855317-5

Bhaskar, R. (2015). *The possibility of naturalism: A philosophical critique of the contemporary human sciences (4th ed.).* Routledge.

Bosman, J., Bruno, I., Chapman, C., Tzovaras, B. G., Jacobs, N., Kramer, B., Martone, M. E., Murphy, F., O'Donnell, D. P., Bar-Sinai, M., Hagstrom, S., Utley, J., & Veksler, L. (2017). *The scholarly commons—Principles and practices to guide research communication.* OSF Preprints. https://osf.io/6c2xt/

Bourdieu, P. (1979). *Distinction: A social critique of the judgement of taste.* Routledge.

Burr, V. (2015). *Social constructionism (3rd ed.).* Routledge. 10.4324/9781315 715421

Elder-Vass, D. (2012). *The reality of social construction.* Cambridge University Press.

Elder-Vass, D. (2021). Critical realism. In G. Delanty & S. Turner (Eds.), *Routledge international handbook of contemporary social and political theory* (2nd ed., pp. 241–249). Routledge.

Elder-Vass, D. (2022). Pragmatism, critical realism and the study of value. *Journal of Critical Realism, 21*(3), 261–287. 10.1080/14767430.2022.2049088

Frischmann, B. M., Madison, M. J., & Strandburg, K. J. (Eds.). (2014). *Governing knowledge commons.* Oxford University Press. 10.1093/acprof:oso/9780199972 036.001.0001

Groff, R. (2004). *Critical realism, post-positivism and the possibility of knowledge.* Routledge. 10.4324/9780203417270

Havemann, J., Bezuidenhout, L., Achampong, J., Akligoh, H., Ayodele, O., Hussein, S., Ksibi, N., Mboa Nkoudou, T. H., Obanda, J., Owango, J., Sanga, V. L., Stirling, J., & Wenzelmann, V. (2020). *Harnessing the open science infrastructure for an efficient African response to COVID-19.* Zenodo. 10.5281/ ZENODO.3733768

Hess, C., & Ostrom (Eds.). (2007). *Understanding knowledge as a commons: From theory to practice.* MIT Press.

Johnson, R. (2019). From coalition to commons: Plan S and the future of scholarly communication. *Insights: The UKSG Journal, 32*(1). 10.1629/uksg.453

Larivière, V., & Sugimoto, C. R. (2018). Do authors comply when funders enforce open access to research? *Nature, 562*(7728), 483–486. 10.1038/d41586-018-07101-w

Lewis, P. (2021). Elinor's Ostrom's 'realist orientation': An investigation of the ontological commitments of her analysis of the possibility of self-governance. *Journal of Economic Behavior & Organization, 189*, 623–636. 10.1016/j.jebo.2021.07.021

Mannathukkaren, N. (2010). Postcolonialism and modernity: A critical realist critique. *Journal of Critical Realism, 9*(3), 299–327. 10.1558/jcr.v9i3.299

Maxwell, J. A., & Mittapalli, K. (2010). Realism as a stance for mixed methods research. In *SAGE Handbook of Mixed Methods in Social & Behavioral Research* (pp. 145–168). SAGE. 10.4135/9781506335193.n6

Mboa Nkoudou, T. H. (2020). Epistemic alienation in African scholarly communications: Open access as a pharmakon. In M. P. Eve & J. Gray (Eds.), *Reassembling scholarly communications: Histories, infrastructures, and global politics of open access.* MIT Press. 10.7551/mitpress/11885.003.0006

McGrath, A. E. (2019). *The territories of human reason: Science and theology in an age of multiple rationalities.* Oxford University Press.

Miedema, F. (2022). *Open science: The very idea.* Springer Netherlands. 10.1007/978-94-024-2115-6

Moosavi, L. (2020). The decolonial bandwagon and the dangers of intellectual decolonisation. *International Review of Sociology, 30*(2), 332–354. 10.1080/03906701.2020.1776919

Oreskes, N. (2019). *Why trust science?* Princeton University Press.

Piron, F. (2018). Postcolonial open access. In U. Herb & J. Schopfel (Eds.), *Open divide: Critical studies in open access.* Litwin Books. http://hdl.handle.net/20.500.11794/16178

Sarker, A., & Blomquist, W. (2019). Addressing misperceptions of governing the commons. *Journal of Institutional Economics, 15*(2), 281–301. 10.1017/S1744137418000103

Sayer, A. (2000). *Realism and social science.* SAGE.

Smith, C. (2010). *What is a person? Rethinking humanity, social life, and the moral good from the person up.* University of Chicago Press.

Vickers, E. (2020). Critiquing coloniality, 'epistemic violence' and western hegemony in comparative education – the dangers of ahistoricism and positionality. *Comparative Education, 56*(2), 165–189. 10.1080/03050068.2019.1665268

Waisbich, L. T., Roychoudhury, S., & Haug, S. (2021). Beyond the single story: 'Global South' polyphonies. *Third World Quarterly, 42*(9), 2086–2095. 10.1080/01436597.2021.1948832

Wright, A. (2014). *Christianity and critical realism: Ambiguity, truth and theological literacy.* Routledge.

8 Participatory openness and enabling inclusion

I now want to go on to make the case for participatory openness. Participatory openness needs to work synergistically with scientific and epistemic openness. The case for this form of openness comes last in the argument set out in this book, but it is not of lesser importance. Participatory openness is, in fact, crucial for achieving more equitable and effective open access. It is an important way of addressing participatory and testimonial injustices that occur in the research system. However, achieving participatory openness requires significant change in approaches to scholarly communication, and reshaping of incentive and reward structures in the academy. Many of the changes required are far-reaching, beyond the territory of open access and open science, and so, I will argue, they can only be achieved through concerted and sustained effort involving a wide range of actors in the research system. After dealing with a key contextual epistemic issue, I will focus the discussion in this chapter initially on open access. I will then widen the focus progressively by talking about open science, followed by scholarly communication in general, and then participatory issues in the broader research system. Whilst discussing these wider issues, I will keep the connections with OA in view. A good number of the practice-related issues covered in this chapter have received a lot of attention in recent debates on open access, so there is no need for me to rehearse the arguments in detail here. Rather, my purpose is to outline the key issues briefly, but, importantly, to set them within the context of my overall argument in this book for scientific, epistemic, and participatory openness.

Enabling participation

A system characterised by participatory openness is one that enables the widest range of contributors to and engagements in research, from demographic, geographic and other perspectives. Participatory openness complements scientific and epistemic openness. However, it is possible to

DOI: 10.4324/9781032679259-8

have scientific and epistemic openness without meaningful participatory openness. A form of scientific openness (involving open access, open data, and other open practices) could exist without a wide range of participants contributing to the research. That would result in research outputs produced by only a narrow set of contributors being made openly available (scientific openness without participatory openness). Similarly, epistemic boundaries could be widened, at least to some extent, but without a system which enables geographically, demographically and culturally diverse participation in research (epistemic openness without participatory openness). Participatory openness is therefore necessary in addition to scientific and epistemic openness, and it needs to be developed in its own right, rather than just assuming it will naturally flow from either or both of the others. Of course, different levels or types of participation in any activity or system are possible, but the idea of participatory openness is that there are no unfair limitations on levels or types of participation. The challenge is to ensure participation is genuinely open – that levels or types of participation are not inappropriately limited. Nevertheless, because the case for participatory openness can build conceptually on some of the arguments already discussed in relation to scientific and epistemic openness, we can move ahead more quickly in making the case here.

I have chosen to talk about 'participatory' openness, rather than say 'contributory' openness to emphasise interaction and reciprocity as parts of openness. Leonelli (2023) makes a strong case in the context of open science generally that we should not think of openness as being about "sharing of resources", but rather about processes of interaction, what she calls "judicious connections". The idea of open science as sharing of resources stems, Leonelli argues, from an "object-oriented" view of research, which we should replace with a "process-oriented" view – where openness in research becomes about interaction and exchange. I am similarly emphasising the importance of openness being about participation and interaction. Meaningful participation best happens where there is a shared assumption of equality amongst participants (or minimally, a recognition of mutual participatory legitimacy), and so Leonelli's emphasis on inclusion rather than just sharing is well made. Leonelli argues that inclusion in fact comes before sharing in the logical sequence of open science imperatives. Sharing is, of course, part of interaction, and is important, particularly in relation to open access, but it is not in itself sufficient. I see the different forms of openness that I am advocating – scientific, epistemic, and participatory – as inter-related, and mutually supporting and reinforcing without wanting to arrange them in any prioritised order.

Linking back to the argument in the previous chapter, there is an important epistemic question that needs to be addressed first of all, since it relates to the epistemic grounding of the case for participatory openness in science. As we have seen, some critical and postcolonial accounts of science portray it as 'Western knowledge', a knowledge system which dominates other epistemic systems. This leads to ideas like "epistemicide", and "epistemic alienation" associated with science, and open access as "epistemic poison" (Mboa Nkoudou, 2020). OA, the argument goes, enables an oppressive epistemic system to dominate others. In this book, we have seen that scientific knowledge as it is currently configured is often biased, Eurocentric, and narrow. I have argued that such epistemic problems need to be taken seriously and addressed, despite the considerable practical challenges of doing so.

However, we need to avoid the idea of a dichotomy of modern 'rational' science in the Western tradition pitted against traditional and (by implication) irrational indigenous knowledge. Ironically, such an idea can tend in the direction of recreating the 'orientalist' perspective it purports to be resisting. It seems to involve the same essentialist 'othering', only reversing the favoured side of the dichotomy. The idea that modern science is somehow uniquely Western is problematical in itself – science has a long history outside the West (Poskett, 2022). However, if the idea that science is Western then forms the basis of the argument that non-Western people engaging in science involves them internalising an alien oppressive epistemology, it can ironically become an exclusionary argument. Participation in scientific knowledge production becomes seen as somehow inappropriate and oppressive for people in LMICs. I am resisting this position, as part of my argument for participatory openness, and I am making the case that participation in science should be open to people from LMICs, just as much as HICs. I do not think it should be remarkable to say this. However, it seems it does need saying, since the corollary of the argument that science is an alienating Western discourse, could be that people in LMICs should be excluded from working in science. I am countering that argument. Not only is the contribution to science by people in LMICs a matter of participatory justice, but I am going further in arguing that participatory openness in science is more likely to create conditions where, as we have seen, biases, such as Eurocentrism, can be exposed and addressed (Thorp, 2023). In this way, participatory openness becomes a vehicle for helping to address hermeneutical epistemic injustice, in concert with the epistemic openness I am advocating.

Once we have accepted that people from LMICs should participate in science, and that doing so does not create hermeneutical epistemic injustice in principle, we need to go on to discuss the ways in which the drive for participatory openness can also help to address testimonial epistemic injustice, and wider participatory epistemic injustices (Hookway, 2010), which may prevent people from engaging fairly in scientific activity and scholarly communication. Participatory openness encourages and enables the contribution of people from LMICs to the scientific discourse, voices that have often been less trusted and less valued than others, by dismantling barriers to participation. Testimonial injustice can occur in various ways. Knöchelmann (2021) emphasises the role of peer review and editorial bias in testimonial injustice, where submissions from authors in LMICs can be treated less favourably. Harris et al. (2017) show in a randomised controlled trial involving English clinicians that they rated articles more highly when they believed they originated from HICs as opposed to LICs. In their study of journal peer review in the biological sciences, Smith et al. (2023) found "notably worse review outcomes (for example, lower overall acceptance rates) for authors whose institutional affiliations were in Asia, for authors whose country's primary language is not English and in countries with relatively low Human Development Indices" (Smith et al., 2023, p. 512).

A common response to these kinds of problems is to carry out 'double blind' or 'double anonymous' peer review, where the identity of the author is unknown to the reviewer and vice-versa. Some OA publications practice this approach, as do other many non-OA publications – in fact, there has been a revival in this approach recently aiming to achieve greater equity and inclusion (Conklin & Singh, 2022; Tomkins et al., 2017; Waltman et al., 2022). On the other hand, double-anonymous review can be very difficult to achieve in practice, since in many fields it is difficult, if not impossible, to avoid reviewers recognising authors (Lee et al., 2013). Some AI tools have very high success rates in identifying authorship of anonymised outputs and these and other means of identifying authors are used by at least some reviewers (Bauersfeld et al., 2023). If awareness of identities exists within a framework purporting to be one of anonymity, then there is considerable potential for biases and inequities to be enabled but remain hidden – a worse outcome than exposing them to public view as a matter of policy. Also, double-anonymous peer review is not compatible with sharing of earlier versions of papers (e.g., preprints) or other kinds of open outputs (e.g., datasets) before submission of a paper for peer review, since the anonymity of the submission for peer review would be compromised (Waltman et al., 2022). Double-anonymous peer review thus precludes many open practices prior to the publication of an article.

Some OA advocates therefore favour open peer review, designed to create greater transparency in the peer review process. Open peer review can arguably reduce the likelihood of biases occurring since decision-making is exposed to public scrutiny, making both authors and reviewers accountable for their contributions (Ross-Hellauer, 2017). The worry remains, however, that naming reviewers may discourage them from making highly critical comments, particularly in the case of early-career researchers commenting on the work of late-career researchers, when the latter exercise most power in their subject community. Some would therefore favour reports of reviewers being made open, but not necessarily the identity of reviewers. This is an ongoing debate, and we clearly need more evidence of the effect of different approaches to peer review (including different approaches to naming and anonymity) as a way of designing systems to reduce testimonial injustice.

Open peer review (at least involving open review reports, if not open reviewer identities), along with practices like preprinting, can also form the basis of innovative publishing models, such as the "publish then review" or "publish – review – curate" model, which attempts to reverse the conventional 'review – publish' model of most established journals (Eisen et al., 2020). The aim is to encourage rapid dissemination of content, often using preprint servers, and then for open peer review to be carried out on already-publicly-available content, with the idea that peer review functions primarily to improve the science, not act primarily as gatekeeping (the basis for binary 'accept' or 'reject' decisions) (Eisen et al., 2022). Approaches like this have been present for a long time in the OA discourse, often based on the concept of "overlay journals", which build peer review services on top of preprint servers (Smith, 2000). However, it is interesting to see these sorts of developments now being taken up more widely in practice and it will be important to see whether they have the effect of enabling participation from a more diverse range of researchers.

Such developments may usefully be seen as part of a wider "bibliodiversity" movement (Berger, 2021) – the drive to broaden the range of forms that publishing can take and venues in which it can be located, in order to accommodate different knowledge systems and communication norms. "Bibliodiversity is cultural diversity applied to the world of books. Echoing biodiversity, it refers to the critical diversity of products (books, scripts, eBooks, apps and oral literature) made available to readers" (L'Alliance internationale des éditeurs indépendants quoted in Chan, 2019). Widening the forms by which people can contribute is likely to enable more diverse participation, although this of course creates further challenges about how different forms of communication can be made to work at a global as well as local level.

However, widening global participation in science is not merely a matter of participatory justice, important though that is. It is also a means of achieving greater collective insight, something again linked to the argument for epistemic openness. Greater diversity of perspectives can help address the biases in scientific knowledge that we observed earlier, but perspective diversity can also lead to benefits of better ideas generation and decision-making through 'collective wisdom'. Oreskes

(2019) has demonstrated the importance of diversity in science in order to avoid epistemic blind spots amongst scientists – blind spots which can lead to science going "awry". She explores a range of examples in the history of science (including some recent ones), such as eugenics, rejection of continental drift theory, or limited energy theory – all of which were based on shared assumptions within a demographically narrow scientific community, which had blind spots because it did not welcome different perspectives. Oreskes also observes from historical evidence the tendency of individual scientists to stick with their favoured theories even when there is mounting evidence against them. In this case, it is the scientific community, rather than the individual scientist, that is responsible for making progress in science by replacing old with new or newly adapted theories where the evidence makes it necessary. Scientific knowledge, Oreskes (2019) argues, can most usefully be seen as a collective endeavour, involving a "social epistemology" – an argument militating against a highly individualised view of agency in science favoured, for example, by Popper. There is also a large body of literature that points to the benefits of diversity in groups in improved decision-making (Hong & Page, 2004) which seems to apply to scientific work. In research, there is evidence that research papers with more ethnically diverse authorial teams are more impactful (AlShebli et al., 2018). All this evidence seems to point to the benefits of diversity and inclusiveness in the scientific process and is an important dimension of the case of participatory openness.

Business models and incentive structures

Participatory openness is, I am arguing, an important means of addressing epistemic injustice, particularly testimonial injustice, along with wider issues of participatory injustice. In addition to unfair peer review practices and editorial biases, another important area of debate in relation to OA is exclusionary business models. The APC (article processing charge) business model of gold OA has come under criticism for transferring the problem of unaffordability from readers to authors (Frank et al., 2023), thus creating participatory barriers. APCs may help to solve an access problem but in doing so create a participation problem. Cox (2023) has presented a cogent case that the APC business model creates testimonial epistemic injustice. This is especially the case when Western commercial publishers have used APCs as a way of maintaining high profit margins (Butler et al., 2022), and when APC prices are high and pricing correlates with impact factors (Schönfelder, 2020). Such developments reproduce many of the market dysfunctionalities associated with subscriptions, and make publication in the most prestigious journals the most inaccessible for scholars from low-resource contexts (Mboa Nkoudou, 2020). In a large-scale study of Elsevier journals, Smith et al. (2021) found that "Author Geographic Diversity of OA articles was significantly lower than that of non-OA articles" (p. 1123), apparent evidence of exclusionary effects of APCs. Transformational read-and-publish agreements, which seek to transition subscription-based big deals into OA big deals, are undoubtedly useful as a way of furthering openness rapidly for institutions with existing sizeable library budgets that can be re-purposed to pay transformational agreement fees. However, they do not solve the problems of the unaffordability of OA in LMICs, where aggregate budgets managed by libraries are just as restricted as those for individual APC payments (Bansode & Pujar, 2022). Whilst APC waivers for authors in LMICs are allowed by some publishers, the situation is patchy, and is often criticised as 'grace and favour', maintaining Northern control of the system (Rouhi et al., 2022). Grace and favour can be withdrawn at any time without any accountability and therefore cannot be the basis of a just system.

As we have seen, deploying commons theory in this space may help us to rethink scholarly communication within a community-based self-governing frame. Willinsky (2018) has characterised different approaches in the OA market as either "cooperative" or "commercial paths" to OA. It is notable that many journals and other scholarly communication services produced in LMICs are based on a knowledge commons or cooperative model, as opposed to a knowledge market or commercial model. They are published in a diamond OA form within the academy. This approach has arguably made the transition to OA easier in many LMICs. In South America, for example, the well-established community-based approach to OA was itself founded on a pre-existing infrastructure of journals published and managed within the academy (Debat & Babini, 2020; Packer, 2020; Packer et al., 2014). In contrast, many learned societies and institutions in Western countries have historically seen their publications as a way of generating income, and this has arguably hampered the transition to OA, and particularly more equitable forms of OA (Johnson & Fosci, 2015; Johnson, 2005; Velterop, 2003). However, diamond OA and innovative OA publishing platforms (often involving the publish – review – curate approach) seem to be experiencing growing interest in Western countries (Becerril et al., 2021; Bosman et al., 2021; Dufour et al., 2023). It will be interesting to see whether this represents the beginning of an anti-APC turn in the OA movement in HICs and what sustainable business models can be designed to replace APCs.

However, even when a large amount of literature from LMICs is already openly available, as it is, one of the key current problems is its functional invisibility. Established bibliographic databases, such as Web of Science (WoS) and Scopus often do not include literature from LMICs (Havemann et al., 2020). WoS in particular is often valued for its selectivity and the filtering function it performs, even though that filtering is often problematic from an equity perspective. There are clear biases in its selectivity – biases towards English-language outputs produced in high-resource organisations in Western Europe and North America. To address this, many of the established providers of bibliographic services are working to widen their coverage (Basson et al., 2022), sometimes to counter the biases shaping more selective approaches. Newer services, such as OpenAlex, have much wider coverage. Achieving bibliographic visibility is an essential part of encouraging participatory openness. Doing so will also further illustrate the point made earlier that OA is not a Global North phenomenon being imposed on the Global South. Many non-Western journals and other kinds of research publications, are OA and have been for some time (Van Noorden, 2019).

Bibliographic invisibility has far-reaching consequences. Inclusion in selective bibliographic sources is taken as a sign of quality. It is striking the extent to which perceptions in the research community worldwide of valuable research knowledge are informed by bibliographic databases, like Web of Science. Valuable knowledge becomes seen as that which is in WoS, and within WoS, the relative importance of journal titles is determined by Journal Impact Factors. The value of individual articles is seen as linked with the impact factor of the journal in which it is published. Because of the association of quality with inclusion in WoS, Scopus, and similar databases, and impact factors or equivalent, many evaluation and reward systems in academia are based on these metrics, in HICs and LMICs alike (Arabi et al., 2023; Nassiri-Ansari & McCoy, 2023). In some countries, scientists have been directly rewarded for publishing in journals indexed by WoS or Scopus (Xu et al., 2021). Rankings of journals influenced by WoS and Scopus and impact factors or equivalent are common, and academics are encouraged to publish mainly in those highly-ranked titles (Kulczycki et al., 2022). In many countries, articles in journals indexed by WoS or Scopus are implicitly accepted as higher quality in appointment, promotion and evaluation processes (McKiernan et al., 2019).

This has a profound effect on the behavioural incentives of scientists, creating a strong impetus to publish in journals with high-impact factors listed in major bibliographic databases, to accrue status in the academic reputation economy, and to achieve tenure or promotion (Paulus et al., 2015). Piron et al (2021) point out the negative consequences of this system, particularly for those in LMICs, and also observe that institutional rankings and similar systems of evaluation are often driven by WoS data, disadvantaging institutions as well as individual scientists, and once again skewing behavioural incentives for scientists. The system becomes a vicious circle, with many scientists based in LMICs being pressured to publish work in journals producing English-language content, indexed in Web of Science, but this, in turn, reinforces the dominant position of those titles, and creates an inertia in the system which dampens down innovations in scholarly communication and strengthens existing evaluation hierarchies, disadvantaging scientists in LMICs and their institutions. Such a system will always disadvantage those apart from researchers in large resource-rich research-intensive institutions.

Restructuring such incentive systems in new ways that ensure fairer global participation is crucial for participatory openness. Doing so is, however, an enormous challenge, but a clear first step must be the de-emphasising of impact factors, and similar crude metrics of journal prestige, as proxy indicators of output quality. It is essential to reverse what amounts to the outsourcing of research evaluation to WoS, Scopus and similar services. In fact, a move away from focusing mostly on any crude indicators of 'excellence' is essential if the incentive structure of researchers is to be reformed (Ma, 2022; Wilsdon, 2016). Many agencies globally are now engaging in major reassessment of their evaluation systems in rewarding researchers with funding, recognition and promotion, often inspired by initiatives like DORA (Declaration on Research Assessment) (Hatch & Curry, 2020; Pontika et al., 2022). Such moves may involve widening notions of research excellence in the area of publications to incorporate other indicators, including indicators of openness. In addition, many are attempting to "pluralise" ideas of excellence by moving upstream in the research process from published outputs, to consider questions of research culture and leadership. In addition, agencies are also moving notions of excellence downstream in the research to consider not just academic outputs but also the impact of research on wider society (Jong et al., 2022). Changing the ways evaluation is conducted, for example, introducing different templates for documents presenting research proposals or researcher credentials (e.g., narrative-based CVs) are also potentially important. Such major shifts are challenging both to conceptualise and operationalise, and so require concerted and sustained effort.

Scientific participation beyond open access

Whilst I have focused my argument in this chapter until now on open access issues, it is important to recognise that the drive for participatory openness also applies in many respects to open science more generally, to wider issues associated with scholarly communication (regardless of whether it is OA or not), and also to a broad set of issues with the research system as a whole. I will discuss each of these in turn now. The first issue of open science is important since I would argue that participatory openness can be best achieved when open access is genuinely integrated into a wider open science environment. There is growing awareness of how the different components of open science can operate in an integrated and synergistic way, complementing each other rather than simply co-existing (Besançon et al., 2021). This seems to be reflected in the growth of open science policies, increasingly common in the last decade, rather than just open access ones, which were most common in the first 10–15 years of the 21st century. An obvious example is how sharing datasets that underpin research can complement published papers, providing a more robust and replicable scientific knowledge base. The argument about the importance of bibliographic visibility also points to the need for openness of bibliographic data.

An important aspect of this is infrastructure. Scholarly communication, and research in general, are built on a complex international infrastructure consisting of technologies, processes, protocols, standards, policies, and supporting expertise that enable research workflows, data storage, scholarly communication, and other research activities (Goudarzi & Dunks, 2023). For open access and open science to work, this infrastructure has to be constructed in ways that facilitate openness: for example, using open standards to enable systemic openness (Chan & Mounier, 2019; Gray, 2020; Havemann et al., 2020). There is a real danger that important components of this infrastructure are, like scholarly journals or other scholarly workflow tools, being subjected to commercial enclosure (Brembs et al., 2023; Chen et al., 2019) – awareness of which could usefully give further impetus to 'knowledge commons' approaches in response. Of course, robust infrastructure is not evenly spread globally. As in other areas discussed in this book, we see massive inequities. For example, reliable high-capacity IT networks, which are foundational research infrastructure (and form the basis of much open science activity) are often not consistently present in LMICs (Okafor et al., 2022). Such inequities inhibit participation in science and so addressing them is an important aspect of participatory justice as much as a set of technical challenges.

The drive for participatory openness also leads to challenging questions regarding the role of actors beyond the academy in contributing to scientific knowledge. The benefits of OA in enabling the transfer of scientific knowledge to a wide range of individuals and groups, including businesses, charities and public sector organisations, have been recognised for some time (ElSabry, 2017), but there has been less attention given to contribution to science of those outside the academy, at least in relation to OA. Well-explored ideas of knowledge sharing and exchange, academic engagement and social impact are relevant here (Castaneda & Cuellar, 2020; Perkmann et al., 2021). It could also be argued that the drive to extend research and the reach of research outputs beyond the academy, leads to consideration of citizen science (Hecker et al., 2018). Such participatory approaches to science are designed to break down some of the barriers between the academy and wider society, with mutual knowledge exchange: communicating scientific findings whilst also enabling contributions from outside the academic scientific community. An approach like this, involving an exchange between scientists and those outside the science community, can also be adopted in LMICs when scientists study phenomena in particular contexts, as we saw in Chapter 4. In both HICs and LMICs encouraging wider participation in the research process from beyond the academy can begin to address epistemic objectification.

The challenge of achieving wider participation in science is not just related to the issue of openness, however. There is a whole raft of other problems associated with participation in scholarly communication more generally, which overlap with but are not identical to those associated with OA (Collyer, 2018; Nakamura et al., 2023). Problems relating to authorship are an example. Those involved in producing research based in LMICs in particular may not be given the opportunity to contribute to research outputs, since their involvement may not constitute what is normally considered authorship, or their role as authors may be limited to particular functions, such as data gathering, rather than conceptualisation, theorising and so on (Tankwanchi et al., 2023). Standards like CRediT (Contributor Roles Taxonomy) may help research groups to consider and make transparent the set-up of their authorial team, and are designed to facilitate a move "from authorship to contributorship" (Allen et al., 2019). At the very least, standards like this help to expose problems so that they can then be addressed. Problems of authorial roles are, of course, reflective of much larger issues associated with the setup of collaborative research teams in general. Even where research groups include representatives from HICs and LMICs in the same group, the relationships between them can often be characterised by power asymmetries in favour of those from HICs, with collaborators from HICs often taking a leadership role. This is particularly the case when research funding comes from agencies in HICs, as it often does.

There is the wider problem of recognition of expertise. Nakamura et al. (2023) observe,

Global North researchers are often regarded as experts in their respective fields, enjoying a reputation beyond their local contexts. Conversely, Global South researchers are often perceived as being confined to their own regions, with their scientific authority seen as deriving from the knowledge and expertise originating in the Global North.

(Nakamura et al., 2023, p. 1)

This is often reflected in scholarly communication citation patterns, with authors from HICs being cited more – a proxy of recognition but again impacting on the skewed reward and incentives systems already discussed. This lack of recognition in citation behaviours, as in other sorts of recognition, has considerable consequences for the way disciplines are understood, where important work is seen to be taking place, often reinforcing Northern-centricities (Collyer, 2018; Kwon, 2022). This again tends to be biased towards the already powerful. It has negative consequences for the careers of scientists and their institutions in LMICs, meaning that they are not appropriately recognised and rewarded for their work in their own right, and may often have to collaborate with researchers from HICs to achieve recognition in their field.

There are further participatory inequities reflected in the wider scholarly communication system, apart from open access or open science. The peer review system (regardless of whether or not it is open) is an important part of the system, with reviewers often acting as gatekeepers (Dumlao & Teplitskiy, 2024). There is a skewing of peer reviewer selection, with reviewers from HICs disproportionately carrying out reviews. Vesper (2018) reports,

> *Researchers in leading science locations, such as the United States, the United Kingdom and Japan, write nearly 2 peer reviews per submitted article of their own, compared with about 0.6 peer reviews per submission by those in emerging countries such as China, Brazil, India and Poland.*
>
> (Vesper, 2018)

This perpetuates biases, and also puts the whole system under enormous pressure. Like reviewers, other powerful gatekeeper roles – journal editors, editorial team members, and editorial boards – are often skewed in favour of HICs (Roh et al., 2020), although many publishers have carried out work recently to begin to address this.

There is also the vexed question of language. In the 20th century, English emerged as the international language of science (Montgomery, 2013), undoubtedly linked to imperialist histories. This has created significant linguistic barriers to participation in science (Amano et al., 2023). Not only is the bibliographic record English-biased (e.g., in WoS), but the scientific literature itself is. 'International' publications are normally English-language publications. Whilst an international language of science may improve collaborations and promote mobility in the scientific community, there are major epistemic and practical problems to which it gives rise. Scientists who do not speak English as their first language bear considerable "costs", including spending longer finding and reading literature, writing their own research, and preparing contributions to conferences (Amano et al., 2023). Their work is more likely to be rejected by English-language journals. There is no easy answer to this problem of linguistic exclusion, although there are numerous pragmatic approaches to addressing challenges, including making use of technological developments to help with translation and language enhancement. Nevertheless, a recognition of the ongoing need for greater multilingualism is an important starting point for promoting wider participation.

Participatory problems associated with open access, open science and scholarly communication are, of course, reflective of much bigger problems relating to the wider science system. At the macro level, national participation in global science correlates with national income, and the capacity of a country to fund science cannot be solved by merely extending openness. There are massive problems associated with national research institutions, infrastructures, and policies often linked with wider economic development issues. There are also other important participatory injustices in the system, some reflected in scholarly communication but part of much bigger problems. There are well-documented cases of testimonial injustice relating to gender, for example, with women scientists experiencing discrimination, historically associated with traditional notions of authority (Elder-Vass, 2012, p. 217). Ways in which such injustices interact in relation to say women from indigenous communities based in LMICs are particularly challenging. Like all these systemic challenges there is a need for engagement from across the research system to address them, including all the relevant actor groups (policymakers, funders, publishers, librarians, university managers and so on), representing different disciplinary and professional communities in different locations.

It is important to recognise that what is required is not simply to bring researchers from LMICs into a pre-existing research environment created by HICs, but rather a reorientation of the global research system, including in HICs. Most of the changes for which I am arguing apply just as much to research-performing institutions in high-resource environments as they do to those in low-resource environments. More community-based publishing and less impact-factor-based evaluation are just as important in HICs. Connell (2007) in her account of the transformation required in "Metropolitan" (i.e., Western or Global North) social science talks about necessary personal and structural changes:

> *To change the way metropolitan social science operates in the world requires a retooling that will be arduous and perhaps also expensive. Professional self-images, personal stocks of knowledge, affiliations, citation practices, publication strategies both of individuals and of*

> *publishing houses, grant-getting and practical applications of social science, are all at stake. So is teaching.*
>
> (Connell, 2007, p. 227)

Such a "retooling" is necessary across disciplines and countries in HICs and LMICs. It is necessary at personal and structural levels.

Participatory openness is then an ambitious aim that has implications for open access but also more broadly for open science and scholarly communication, in ways that connect with the scientific endeavour as a whole. Significantly, these approaches are part of a wider agenda that has developed over a quarter of a century or more to make science more participative and societally connected. Gibbons (1999), in an influential agenda-setting essay, argued that science should be more widely participative as part of the "social contract" between science and society. Arguing for the need for a shift from science merely producing "reliable knowledge" to producing "socially robust knowledge", which is credible and socially relevant, Gibbons emphasised this needs a more open and participatory approach to science:

> *Reliable knowledge may have been best produced by such cohesive (and therefore restricted) scientific communities. But socially robust knowledge can only be produced by much more sprawling socio/scientific constituencies with open frontiers.*
>
> (Gibbons, 1999, p. 84)

Gibbons was not talking about open access or open science, but in many respects, the context he discusses in the 1990s is the one in which open access and open science first gained traction. Open access and open science generally are ways in which science can create more "open frontiers" enabling greater transparency and accountability in society.

This brings us full circle to the rationale for greater OA developed since the turn of the 21st century (as discussed in Chapter 3). Transparency and accountability were amongst the key justifications for greater openness in science then, and have been evident in debates since that time. Arguably, the participatory openness for which I am arguing can also be situated in the more general picture painted by Gibbons, alongside scientific openness, where participatory openness extends the frontiers of science to previously marginalised and excluded groups. Participatory openness needs to occur at a global level, across different science systems in different regions. Of course, open access and open science can only get us so far in addressing the massive participatory barriers that exist in global science, but despite the enormous challenges, openness has a role to play in creating greater participatory equity in the research system.

References

Allen, L., O'Connell, A., & Kiermer, V. (2019). How can we ensure visibility and diversity in research contributions? How the Contributor Role Taxonomy (CRediT) is helping the shift from authorship to contributorship. *Learned Publishing, 32*(1), 71–74. 10.1002/leap.1210

AlShebli, B. K., Rahwan, T., & Woon, W. L. (2018). The preeminence of ethnic diversity in scientific collaboration. *Nature Communications, 9*(1), Article 1. 10.1038/s41467-018-07634-8

Amano, T., Ramírez-Castañeda, V., Berdejo-Espinola, V., Borokini, I., Chowdhury, S., Golivets, M., González-Trujillo, J. D., Montaño-Centellas, F., Paudel, K., White, R. L., & Veríssimo, D. (2023). The manifold costs of being a non-native English speaker in science. *PLOS Biology, 21*(7), e3002184. 10.1371/journal.pbio.3002184

Arabi, S., Ni, C., & Hutchins, B. I. (2023). *You do not receive enough recognition for your influential science.* bioRxiv. 10.1101/2023.09.07.556750

Bansode, S. Y., & Pujar, S. (2022). Open access and transformative agreements: A study. *Annals of Library and Information Studies (ALIS), 69*(1), Article 1. 10.56042/alis.v69i1.57094

Basson, I., Simard, M.-A., Ouangré, Z. A., Sugimoto, C. R., & Larivière, V. (2022). The effect of data sources on the measurement of open access: A comparison of Dimensions and the Web of Science. *PLOS ONE, 17*(3), e0265545. 10.1371/journal.pone.0265545

Bauersfeld, L., Romero, A., Muglikar, M., & Scaramuzza, D. (2023). Cracking double-blind review: Authorship attribution with deep learning. *PLoS One, 18*(6), e0287611. 10.1371/journal.pone.0287611

Becerril, A., Bosman, J., Bjørnshauge, L., Frantsvåg, J. E., Kramer, B., Langlais, P.-C., Mounier, P., Proudman, V., Redhead, C., & Torny, D. (2021). *OA diamond journals study. Part 2: Recommendations.* Zenodo. 10.5281/zenodo.4562790

Berger, M. (2021). Bibliodiversity at the centre: Decolonizing open access. *Development and Change, 52*(2), 383–404. 10.1111/dech.12634

Besançon, L., Peiffer-Smadja, N., Segalas, C., Jiang, H., Masuzzo, P., Smout, C., Billy, E., Deforet, M., & Leyrat, C. (2021). Open science saves lives: Lessons from the COVID-19 pandemic. *BMC Medical Research Methodology, 21*(1), 117. 10.1186/s12874-021-01304-y

Bosman, J., Frantsvåg, J. E., Kramer, B., Langlais, P.-C., & Proudman, V. (2021). *OA diamond journals study. Part 1: Findings.* Zenodo. 10.5281/zenodo.4558704

Brembs, B., Huneman, P., Schönbrodt, F., Nilsonne, G., Susi, T., Siems, R., Perakakis, P., Trachana, V., Ma, L., & Rodriguez-Cuadrado, S. (2023). *Replacing academic journals.* 10.5281/zenodo.7643806

Butler, L.-A., Matthias, L., Simard, M.-A., Mongeon, P., & Haustein, S. (2022). *The oligopoly's shift to open access. How for-profit publishers benefit from article processing charges.* Zenodo. 10.5281/zenodo.7057144

Castaneda, D. I., & Cuellar, S. (2020). Knowledge sharing and innovation: A systematic review. *Knowledge and Process Management, 27*(3), 159–173. 10.1002/kpm.1637

Chan, L. (2019). Introduction: Open infrastructure: From monocultures to bibliodiversity. In L. Chan & P. Mounier (Eds.), *Connecting the knowledge commons—From projects to sustainable infrastructure: The 22nd international conference on electronic publishing – Revised selected papers.* OpenEdition Press. 10.4000/books.oep.8999

Chan, L., & Mounier, P. (2019). *Connecting the knowledge commons—From projects to sustainable infrastructure: The 22nd international conference on electronic publishing – Revised selected papers.* OpenEdition Press. http://books.openedition.org/oep/8999

Chen, G., Posada, A., & Chan, L. (2019). Vertical integration in academic publishing: Implications for knowledge inequality. In P. Mounier (Ed.), *Connecting the knowledge commons—From projects to sustainable infrastructure: The 22nd international conference on electronic publishing – revised selected papers.* OpenEdition Press. 10.4000/books.oep.9068

Collyer, F. M. (2018). Global patterns in the publishing of academic knowledge: Global north, global south. *Current Sociology, 66*(1), 56–73. 10.1177/0011392116680020

Conklin, M., & Singh, S. (2022). Triple-blind review as a solution to gender bias in academic publishing, a theoretical approach. *Studies in Higher Education, 47*(12), 2487–2496. 10.1080/03075079.2022.2081681

Connell, R. (2007). *Southern theory: The global dynamics of knowledge in social science.* Polity.

Cox, E. (2023). Research outputs as testimony and the APC as testimonial injustice in the Global South. *College & Research Libraries, 84*(4), 513–530. 10.5860/crl.84.4.513

Debat, H., & Babini, D. (2020). Plan S in Latin America: A precautionary note. *Scholarly and Research Communication, 11*(1). 10.22230/src.2020v11n1a347

Dufour, Q., Pontille, D., & Torny, D. (2023). *Supporting diamond open access journals. Interest and feasibility of direct funding mechanisms.* bioRxiv. 10.1101/2023.05.03.539231

Dumlao, J. M. Z., & Teplitskiy, M. (2024). *Lack of peer reviewer diversity advantages authors from wealthier countries.* OSF. 10.31235/osf.io/754e3

Eisen, M. B., Akhmanova, A., Behrens, T. E., Diedrichsen, J., Harper, D. M., Iordanova, M. D., Weigel, D., & Zaidi, M. (2022). Peer review without gatekeeping. *eLife, 11*, e83889. 10.7554/eLife.83889

Eisen, M. B., Akhmanova, A., Behrens, T. E., Harper, D. M., Weigel, D., & Zaidi, M. (2020). Implementing a 'publish, then review' model of publishing. *eLife, 9*, e64910. 10.7554/eLife.64910

Elder-Vass, D. (2012). *The reality of social construction.* Cambridge University Press.

ElSabry, E. (2017). Who needs access to research? Exploring the societal impact of open access. *Revue Française Des Sciences de l'information et de La Communication, 11.* 10.4000/rfsic.3271

Frank, J., Foster, R., & Pagliari, C. (2023). Open access publishing – Noble intention, flawed reality. *Social Science & Medicine, 317*, 115592. 10.1016/j.socscimed.2022.115592

Gibbons, M. (1999). Science's new social contract with society. *Nature, 402*(6761), Article 6761. 10.1038/35011576

Goudarzi, S., & Dunks, R. (2023). *Defining open scholarly infrastructure: A review of relevant literature.* Zenodo. 10.5281/zenodo.8064102

Gray, J. (2020). Infrastructural experiments and the politics of open access. In E. Martin & J. Gray (Eds.), *Reassembling scholarly communications: Histories, infrastructures, and global politics of open access.* 10.7551/mitpress/11885.003.0026

Harris, M., Marti, J., Watt, H., Bhatti, Y., Macinko, J., & Darzi, A. W. (2017). Explicit bias toward high-income-country research: A randomized, blinded, crossover experiment of English clinicians. *Health Affairs, 36*(11), 1997–2004. 10.1377/hlthaff.2017.0773

Hatch, A., & Curry, S. (2020). Changing how we evaluate research is difficult, but not impossible. *eLife*, *9*, e58654. 10.7554/eLife.58654

Havemann, J., Bezuidenhout, L., Achampong, J., Akligoh, H., Ayodele, O., Hussein, S., Ksibi, N., Mboa Nkoudou, T. H., Obanda, J., Owango, J., Sanga, V. L., Stirling, J., & Wenzelmann, V. (2020). *Harnessing the open science infrastructure for an efficient African response to COVID-19*. Zenodo. 10.5281/ZENODO.3733768

Hecker, S., Haklay, M. E., Bowser, A., Makuch, Z., Vogel, J., & Bonn, A. (2018). *Citizen science: Innovation in open science, society and policy* (S. Hecker, M. E. Haklay, A. Bowser, Z. Makuch, J. Vogel, & A. Bonn, Eds.). UCL Press. 10.14324/111.9781787352339

Hong, L., & Page, S. E. (2004). Groups of diverse problem solvers can outperform groups of high-ability problem solvers. *Proceedings of the National Academy of Sciences*, *101*(46), 16385–16389. 10.1073/pnas.0403723101

Hookway, C. (2010). Some varieties of epistemic injustice: Reflections on Fricker. *Episteme*, *7*(2), 151–163. 10.3366/epi.2010.0005

Johnson, R., & Fosci, M. (2015). On shifting sands: Assessing the financial sustainability of UK learned societies. *Learned Publishing*, *28*(4), 274–282. 10.1087/20150406

Johnson, R. K. (2005). Open access: Unlocking the value of scientific research. *Journal of Library Administration*, *42*(2), 107–124. 10.1300/J111v42n02_08

Jong, L., Franssen, T., & Pinfield, S. (2022). *Transforming excellence? From 'matter of fact' to 'matter of concern' in research funding organizations*. 10.31235/osf.io/nduxf

Knöchelmann, M. (2021). The democratisation myth: Open access and the solidification of epistemic injustices. *Science & Technology Studies*, *34*(2), Article 2. 10.23987/sts.94964

Kulczycki, E., Huang, Y., Zuccala, A. A., Engels, T. C. E., Ferrara, A., Guns, R., Pölönen, J., Sivertsen, G., Taşkın, Z., & Zhang, L. (2022). Uses of the journal impact factor in national journal rankings in China and Europe. *Journal of the Association for Information Science and Technology*, *73*(12), 1741–1754. 10.1002/asi.24706

Kwon, D. (2022). The rise of citational justice: How scholars are making references fairer. *Nature*, *603*(7902), 568–571. 10.1038/d41586-022-00793-1

Lee, C. J., Sugimoto, C. R., Zhang, G., & Cronin, B. (2013). Bias in peer review. *Journal of the American Society for Information Science and Technology*, *64*(1), 2–17. 10.1002/asi.22784

Leonelli, S. (2023). *Philosophy of open science*. Cambridge University Press. 10.1017/9781009416368

Ma, L. (2022). Metrics and epistemic injustice. *Journal of Documentation*, *78*(7), 392–404. 10.1108/JD-12-2021-0240

Mboa Nkoudou, T. H. (2020). Epistemic alienation in African scholarly communications: Open access as a pharmakon. In M. P. Eve, & J. Gray (Eds.), *Reassembling scholarly communications: Histories, infrastructures, and global politics of open access*. MIT Press. 10.7551/mitpress/11885.003.0006

McKiernan, E. C., Schimanski, L. A., Nieves, C. M., Matthias, L., Niles, M. T., & Alperin, J. P. (2019). *Use of the Journal Impact Factor in academic review, promotion, and tenure evaluations*. 10.7287/peerj.preprints.27638v2

Montgomery, S. L. (2013). *Does science need a global language? English and the future of research*. The University of Chicago Press.

Nakamura, G., Soares, B. E., Pillar, V. D., Diniz-Filho, J. A. F., & Duarte, L. (2023). Three pathways to better recognize the expertise of Global South researchers. *Npj Biodiversity*, *2*(1), Article 1. 10.1038/s44185-023-00021-7

Nassiri-Ansari, T., & McCoy, D. (2023). *World-class universities? Interrogating the biases and coloniality of global university rankings*. United Nations University - International Institute for Global Health (UNU - IIGH). https://collections.unu.edu/view/UNU:9082?s=03#viewMetadata

Okafor, I. A., Mbagwu, S. I., Chia, T., Hasim, Z., Udokanma, E. E., & Chandran, K. (2022). Institutionalizing open science in Africa: Limitations and prospects. *Frontiers in Research Metrics and Analytics, 7*. https://www.frontiersin.org/articles/10.3389/frma.2022.855198

Oreskes, N. (2019). *Why trust science?* Princeton University Press.

Packer, A. (2020). The pasts, presents, and futures of SciELO. In M. P. Eve & J. Gray (Eds.), *Reassembling scholarly communications: Histories, infrastructures, and global politics of open access* (pp. 297–313). MIT Press. 10.7551/mitpress/11885.003.0030

Packer, A., Cop, N., Luccisano, A., Ramalho, A., & Spinak, E. (2014). *SciELO - 15 years of open access: An analytic study of open access and scholarly communication*. UNESCO. 10.7476/9789230012373

Paulus, F. M., Rademacher, L., Schäfer, T. A. J., Müller-Pinzler, L., & Krach, S. (2015). Journal impact factor shapes scientists' reward signal in the prospect of publication. *PLoS One, 10*(11), e0142537. 10.1371/journal.pone.0142537

Perkmann, M., Salandra, R., Tartari, V., McKelvey, M., & Hughes, A. (2021). Academic engagement: A review of the literature 2011-2019. *Research Policy, 50*(1), 104114. 10.1016/j.respol.2020.104114

Piron, F., Olyhoek, T., Vilchis, I. L., Smith, I., & Liré, Z. (2021). Saying 'no' to rankings and metrics: Scholarly communication and knowledge democracy. In B. L. Hall & R. Tandon (Eds.), *Socially responsible higher education* (pp. 80–91). Brill. 10.1163/9789004459076_007

Pontika, N., Klebel, T., Correia, A., Metzler, H., Knoth, P., & Ross-Hellauer, T. (2022). Indicators of research quality, quantity, openness, and responsibility in institutional review, promotion, and tenure policies across seven countries. *Quantitative Science Studies, 3*(4), 888–911. 10.1162/qss_a_00224

Poskett, J. (2022). *Horizons: A global history of science*. Viking.

Roh, C., Harrison, F. I., & Dabrinski, E. (2020). Scholarly communications and social justice. In M. P. Eve, & J. Gray (Eds.), *Reassembling scholarly communications: Histories, infrastructures, and global politics of open access*. MIT Press. 10.7551/mitpress/11885.003.0007

Ross-Hellauer, T. (2017). What is open peer review? A systematic review. *F1000Research, 6*, 588. 10.12688/f1000research.11369.1

Rouhi, S., Beard, R., & Brundy, C. (2022). Left in the cold: The failure of APC waiver programs to provide author equity. *Science Editor, 45*, 5–13. 10.36591/SE-D-4501-5

Schönfelder, N. (2020). Article processing charges: Mirroring the citation impact or legacy of the subscription-based model? *Quantitative Science Studies, 1*(1), 6–27. 10.1162/qss_a_00015

Smith, A. (2000). The journal as an overlay on preprint databases. *Learned Publishing, 13*(1), 43–48. 10.1087/09531510050145542

Smith, A. C., Merz, L., Borden, J. B., Gulick, C. K., Kshirsagar, A. R., & Bruna, E. M. (2021). Assessing the effect of article processing charges on the geographic diversity of authors using Elsevier's "Mirror Journal" system. *Quantitative Science Studies, 2*(4), 1123–1143. 10.1162/qss_a_00157

Smith, O. M., Davis, K. L., Pizza, R. B., Waterman, R., Dobson, K. C., Foster, B., Jarvey, J. C., Jones, L. N., Leuenberger, W., Nourn, N., Conway, E. E., Fiser, C. M., Hansen, Z. A., Hristova, A., Mack, C., Saunders, A. N., Utley, O. J., Young, M. L., & Davis, C. L. (2023). Peer review perpetuates barriers for historically excluded groups. *Nature Ecology & Evolution, 7*(4), 512–523. 10.1038/s41559-023-01999-w

Tankwanchi, A. S., Asabor, E. N., & Vermund, S. H. (2023). Global health perspectives on race in research: Neocolonial extraction and local marginalization. *International Journal of Environmental Research and Public Health, 20*(13), Article 13. 10.3390/ijerph20136210

Thorp, H. H. (2023, May 11). It matters who does science. *Science Editor's Blog.* https://www.science.org/content/blog-post/it-matters-who-does-science

Tomkins, A., Zhang, M., & Heavlin, W. D. (2017). Reviewer bias in single- versus double-blind peer review. *Proceedings of the National Academy of Sciences, 114*(48), 12708–12713. 10.1073/pnas.1707323114

Van Noorden, R. (2019, May). Indonesia tops open-access publishing charts. *Nature.* 10.1038/d41586-019-01536-5

Velterop, J. (2003). Should scholarly societies embrace open access (or is it the kiss of death)? *Learned Publishing, 16*(3), 167–169. 10.1087/09531510332211 0932

Vesper, I. (2018). Peer reviewers unmasked: Largest global survey reveals trends. *Nature.* 10.1038/d41586-018-06602-y

Waltman, L., Kaltenbrunner, W., Pinfield, S., & Woods, H. B. (2022). *How to improve scientific peer review: Four schools of thought.* SocArXiv. 10.31235/osf.io/v8ghj

Willinsky, J. (2018). The academic library in the face of cooperative and commercial paths to open access. *Library Trends, 67*(2), 196–213. 10.1353/lib.2018.0033

Wilsdon, J. (2016). *The metric tide: The independent review of the role of metrics in research assessment and management.* Sage.

Xu, X., Rose, H., & Oancea, A. (2021). Incentivising international publications: Institutional policymaking in Chinese higher education. *Studies in Higher Education, 46*(6), 1132–1145. 10.1080/03075079.2019.1672646

9 Conclusion

The need for scientific, epistemic, and participatory openness

At the beginning of this book, I identified three related critiques of open access with which I have now engaged. First was the critique that business models associated with OA are often exploitative and exclusionary. Second was the critique that incentive structures in the academy, reinforced by OA, constrain or restrict participation from less-well-funded institutions and regions, including low- and middle-income countries. Third was the critique that knowledge systems of the Global North enabled by OA are being imposed on the Global South, marginalising indigenous knowledges.

I have argued that the first two critiques identify issues needing urgent and sustained attention. Certain modes of OA have become or are becoming exploitive and unaffordable, and these have contributed to the reinforcing of systemic barriers to participation in scholarly communication. I have argued that reward and evaluation systems in research are often exclusionary. There is a need to recast approaches to openness, learning from community-based models developed in LMICs, and to combine these with root-and-branch change in evaluation and incentive systems. Doing so is, of course, enormously challenging and requires concerted action. I have suggested areas where some of this action can focus, including, for example, moving away from highly commercialised APC-based business models for publishing, and from evaluation and reward systems based on crude metrics from selective bibliographic databases.

In relation to the third critique, I have argued that there is a clear need to address problems of bias and particularism embedded in science. This should be done, however, without losing sight of the value of science and the importance of sharing scientific findings. Science, in the broadest sense of that term to mean systematic knowledge, can create enormous benefits for society. Moreover, the contribution of science can be enhanced, I have argued, if it is brought into meaningful conversation with other knowledge systems. However, that does not mean we have to relativise away the importance of science, or indeed other knowledge

DOI: 10.4324/9781032679259-9

systems. Instead, it is essential we maintain ways of discerning between the merits of different knowledge claims where they are in competition, whatever knowledge system they are from. Doing so, in fact, is an endeavour central to research and scholarly communication.

My argument has been that scientific openness (open access to research outputs, open data, and so on) is necessary but not sufficient to achieve more equitable and effective scholarly communication globally. Scientific openness needs to be accompanied by epistemic openness and participatory openness. At the heart of the open access movement are the key issues of what constitutes valid and valuable knowledge, how we know, and who gets to say. I have argued that an approach that combines greater scientific openness with epistemic openness and participatory openness is needed to make progress on these issues. Scientific openness works where the content, processes and infrastructure of research are made openly available. Epistemic openness operates when different kinds of knowledge and knowledge systems are valued and engaged with across and beyond conventional science. Participatory openness exists when as many participants as possible are brought into the conversation and are fully involved in ongoing scientific interactions. Scientific openness, epistemic openness, and participatory openness are interrelated, mutually supporting and mutually reinforcing.

The different forms of openness for which I have argued can work together to produce a more effective and equitable global scholarly communication system, and make contributions to a more effective and equitable research system. Both are important – effectiveness and equity. The effectiveness of the system, designed to enable the communication of science widely and in a timely way, will be enhanced by the reduction in systemic friction. Information can then be shared, scrutinised, critiqued, refined, and built on without the unnecessary restrictions and constraints inherent in conventional approaches to research and scholarly communication, such as subscription paywalls. The equity of the system will be enhanced by valuing different perspectives and contributions from a wide range of active participants, without the exclusions commonly seen currently. Scientific openness when complemented by epistemic and participatory openness, I have argued, can expose epistemic particularism to scrutiny and critique. Effectiveness and equity, I have suggested, can be enhanced through redesigning business and sustainability models underpinning open-access services. I have advocated a greater emphasis on a knowledge commons approach, exemplified by several publication platforms in LMICs, and a consequent move away from the knowledge market approach. Community-based publishing and dissemination rather than highly commercialised approaches are more likely to lead to greater effectiveness and equity in the scholarly communication system.

I have suggested that current debates about openness are often based on divergent meta-theoretical positions, without that being sufficiently acknowledged. Advocates and critics of OA often talk past each other, using different conceptual frames and languages, and it has been important to explore these differences at some length. Advocates of OA have often based their arguments on positivist or adapted-positivist paradigms and liberal social theory, and critics of OA often base their arguments on critical social theory informed by radical constructionism. The fact their arguments use these different paradigms often hampers meaningful dialogue.

I have proposed that a critical realist social constructionism can provide a robust undergirding for consideration of these questions. Critical realism accommodates a moderate constructionism, which is a necessary grounding for epistemic openness, in opposition to the narrow epistemology of positivism. The idea of epistemic openness (recognition of the validity and value of different knowledge forms) makes little sense in positivist meta-theory. At the same time, a critical realist approach, with its emphasis on judgemental rationality, ensures that relativism and incommensurability problems associated with radical constructionism can be avoided, making scientific and participatory openness meaningful. Radical constructionism tends to relativise away the value of science, making scientific openness at best of limited value and, at worst, oppressive. The idea of scientific knowledge as a form of Northern oppression can also have an exclusionary effect: discouraging widespread participation in science. In contrast, epistemic openness allows different ideas to be contributed, compared and critiqued as part of a globally shared knowledge commons. This does not mean anything goes, however. Rather, the combination of the idea of epistemological relativism with judgemental rationality means that ongoing discussion and debate are essential for discerning the best explanations – something, I have argued, which is enabled by OA, in that OA makes the different contributions to the scholarly discourse available as widely as possible.

Critical realism also comes with the idea of "laminated reality", to which different layers of explanation derived from different kinds of knowledge can usefully contribute. Social theory based on or compatible with critical realism, I have suggested, can provide considerable explanatory insight in taking forward the open agenda and in demonstrating the benefits of openness. I have discussed the potential that commons theory has in this area. I have also emphasised the need for sensitivity and humility in carrying out discussion and debate.

Resting on this meta-theoretical foundation is the idea of social justice, the importance of which I have emphasised throughout this book. In many respects, my argument for openness can be summarised with reference to the theory of epistemic justice, an important aspect of social justice. I have argued that open access has the potential to address distributive epistemic injustice, by contributing to a more just distribution of informational and educational resources. I have suggested that has always been an implicit aim of the OA movement. However, it has been fundamental to my argument that to address distributive injustice meaningfully, open access needs to be developed in ways that also recognise discriminatory epistemic injustice, particularly hermeneutical and testimonial epistemic injustices. My argument for epistemic openness has largely been framed in a way that aims to counter hermeneutical epistemic injustice: creating an environment in which contributions from different epistemic systems are welcomed. My argument for participatory openness has related strongly to ways of addressing testimonial injustice: creating an environment in which different voices are heard and valued. Participatory openness can also help eradicate objectification in research, with different communities contributing to research, not just acting as the objects of study. The case I have made has, therefore, balanced the need to address discriminatory epistemic injustice with the need to continue to work on OA as a means of achieving greater distributive epistemic justice.

I have indicated, albeit briefly, that such an approach can be the basis of an ethical case for open access. An ethical case for open access, in other words, can start with its role in furthering epistemic justice: in addressing (or beginning to address) both distributive and discriminatory epistemic injustice. Addressing distributive epistemic injustice (the unfair distribution of informational and educational resources), which OA has often been implicitly designed to do, can be one form of a movement to address wider global distributive injustices. Addressing discriminatory epistemic injustice (hermeneutical and testimonial injustices), alongside other participatory epistemic injustices, which I have argued OA can help to do, can contribute to wider anti-discrimination moves as part of a larger global social justice movement. Working towards greater social justice through addressing distributive and discriminatory epistemic injustice through OA is part of a much bigger picture of social justice, to which OA can contribute.

This idea of justice has important social (or systemic) dimensions as well as personal (or agential) dimensions. For example, addressing discriminatory epistemic injustice – allowing a variety of voices to be heard and enabling different perspectives to be valued and interactions to be welcomed – has important individual and social implications. Implicit in my argument has been an understanding of justice that combines these personal and collective layers. As with social theory, notions of justice can often be highly individualised or highly collectivised. I am arguing in relation to justice, just as I did in relation to social theory, that we need to combine the agential and structural, the personal and social. Distributive justice and anti-discriminatory justice relate to both people and communities, in their social and cultural settings, as both receivers and contributors. Addressing both these levels (personal and social) and both roles (receivers and contributors) can have a dialogic effect, with openness being characterised by sharing and collaboration. These and other aspects of the ethical case for open access merit further elaboration and discussion on another occasion. They remind us that open access is not an end in itself. Open science is not an end in itself. Both are designed to make the science system work more effectively and more equitably so that science itself can contribute positively to society.

Although I have focused mainly on open access in scholarly communication, I believe my arguments on scientific openness (of which OA is a part) apply in many respects to open science more generally. Arguments for scientific, epistemic, and participatory openness apply just as much when discussing open data or open peer review, for example. Open data can be a valuable form of participation in scientific discourse in its own right, which can enhance the intelligibility of reported research findings. Open peer review can, in the right circumstances, increase accountability and expose biases and ethnocentricities. My argument is consistent with the fact that the different components of open science are, I believe, increasingly being recognised as synergistic.

The role played by open access and open science in addressing daunting global problems of inequity and exclusion, of course, needs to be kept in perspective – I have tried to avoid over-claiming the importance of openness amongst a vast array of developments needed to address global challenges. The problems are large and complex, and often seem intractable. However, my argument has been that open access and open science have a role to play, and the role they do play in the global scientific system has the potential to be transformative in science and how science can make a positive contribution to wider society.

Nevertheless, in order to move ahead as I have suggested, open access itself, and open science more generally, need to change. What I have discussed in this book, addresses some of the changes that are needed if openness is to achieve its potential. We have seen some recent policy initiatives, such as the UNESCO Open Science Recommendation (UNESCO, 2021), and new drives towards innovative and community-based publishing models, changing open access in ways likely to make it more effective and equitable. We began this book by looking at the Budapest Open Access Initiative statement (BOAI, 2002) as a touchstone of the OA movement. Despite its continued importance in this role, the BOAI agenda has itself been progressed. In a statement released marking the 20th anniversary of the BOAI (2022), many of its original framers endorsed the UNESCO Recommendation on Open Science, with UNESCO's emphasis on the four "pillars" of OS, which comprise open knowledge and open infrastructure, and also connections between science and society, and links between science and other epistemic systems. BOAI@20 emphasised the continued need for greater openness as a means of improving science and achieving societal benefits, and doing so in ways that minimise the dangers of creating new inequities and exclusions. We can now see that, as OA becomes genuinely global, this is more important than ever. However, the original aims of the BOAI of improving access to and impact of scientific work through openness, thus promoting a global knowledge-based "conversation", are aims that need to remain at the heart of open access.

None of this is easy. Many barriers remain. In trying to address them, it is important we critique ways in which OA has often been implemented. We need to face up to the fact that some OA implementations have reinforced exclusions and inequities. That has been one feature of this book. However, this book has also been about exploring how a reshaped form of openness can enable a better scholarly communication system and contribute to a better global science system. If open access is to deliver its potential, I have argued, then scientific openness needs to be combined with epistemic openness and participatory openness so that together they can enable a system that is both more effective and equitable.

References

BOAI. (2002). *Budapest open access initiative.* http://www.budapestopen accessinitiative.org/read

BOAI. (2022). *Budapest open access initiative: 20th anniversary recommendations.* https://www.budapestopenaccessinitiative.org/boai20/

UNESCO. (2021). *UNESCO recommendation on open science.* UNESCO. https://unesdoc.unesco.org/ark:/48223/pf0000379949.locale=en

Index